THE
THIRTEENTH
FLOOR

How Dealing With Trauma
Transformed My Approach
to Employee Well-Being

CARLY FLIESHER

LEGACY
launch pad
PUBLISHING

DISCLAIMER

This work is non-fiction and, as such, reflects the author's memory of her experiences. Many of the names and identifying characteristics of the individuals featured in this book have been changed to protect their privacy and certain individuals are composites. Dialogue and events have been recreated; in some cases, conversations have been edited to convey their substance rather than written exactly as they occurred.

For more information about Carly Fliesher,
scan the QR code below:

DEDICATION

To Kevin, Olivia and Logan

INTRODUCTION

The 13th floor of a Las Vegas hotel isn't supposed to exist, but I slept there anyway. As a Southern Californian, Vegas had become my retreat—a destination for getaways, girls' weekends and concerts.

As we drove along the highway and I watched Las Vegas emerge on the horizon, anticipation built. In the car, I sat beside my husband Kevin, my best friend Lauren and her husband Chris. This would be my second Route 91 Harvest Festival, where Sam Hunt, Eric Church and Jason Aldean would be playing.

We pulled up to the Tropicana Hotel instead of our initially planned Mandalay Bay. One of our friends had backed out at the last minute, prompting the change. The Tropicana stood directly across from the festival grounds—convenient for moving between shows.

The casino floor buzzed with activity as we entered

—slot machines ringing, people laughing and glasses clinking. The worn carpet beneath my feet revealed an older Vegas establishment. "We're here to check in," I said to the receptionist, sliding our IDs across the counter.

She tapped at her computer, then looked up with a smile. "You'll be staying on floor 13, I mean 14," she corrected herself, handing over our room keys with directions to the elevator.

A chill snaked up my spine. 13th floor. Hotels typically skipped labeling the 13th floor due to superstition. Uneasiness settled in my stomach, but I pushed it away, focusing instead on the weekend ahead.

$\sim$

The bass pounded through my chest as we approached the festival entrance on the first night, Tommy Bahama chairs slung over our shoulders. Excitement rippled through the crowd around us as we prepared for Eric Church to perform.

"Security's probably going to be tight," I whispered to Lauren, nervously patting the hidden flask we were attempting to smuggle in.

Metal detectors stood at the entry point. An attendant directed us to set our chairs aside for checking while we walked through the detector frame.

Beep.

We passed through without incident, collected our chairs and moved into the venue.

"That was easy," I muttered to Lauren. "I could have had a gun or a knife in there."

She nodded, her expression mirroring my concern. "Yeah, that's...weird."

The uneasiness returned, sitting heavy in my chest even as Eric Church took the stage and the crowd erupted in cheers.

On day two, Sam Hunt came to the stage. I'd been dying to see him live for years.

"He looks just like you." I nudged Kevin playfully as Sam's voice carried across the festival grounds.

But even as I swayed to the music, certain things kept catching my attention—unusual flashing lights from one of the surrounding hotels, the continued lax security. Each time I'd begin to relax, something would tug at the edge of my awareness.

~

"God bless America, land that I love..." The crowd's voices merged on the third night as Big and Rich closed their set. Lighters waved in the darkness. Strangers became friends, united in song. For a moment, music washed away my lingering worry.

The stage went dark in preparation for Jason Aldean's headlining performance.

"I'm heading back to the room." Lauren leaned over, her voice competing with the crowd's excited chatter. "We've seen Jason plenty of times, and I'm exhausted."

Kevin rubbed his temple beside me. "I've got a killer headache. Maybe we should go back too?"

I felt my face flush with irritation. "Just go! I'll be fine. The hotel is right across the street."

"No," he insisted, his eyes meeting mine. "If you're staying, I'll stay. I'm not going to leave you here."

His concern only fueled my irritation. I'd had a few drinks by then and wanted to dance the night away. Having him stay just for me, visibly in pain, made me feel like a burden.

I walked away from Kevin and our friends in the chair corral area, making my way to the dance floor as Jason Aldean took the stage. "Bar Stool Town" poured through the speakers as I lost myself in the rhythm, determined to enjoy the final act of the weekend.

Then a strange sound filtered through the music.

Pop-pop-pop-pop.

I looked up, confused, as Jason and his band suddenly bolted from the stage. The lights cut out, plunging us into darkness.

Is this part of the show? I wondered, waiting for spotlights or pyrotechnics.

Pop-pop-pop-pop-pop.

Realization crawled over me like ice water. *Those are gunshots,* I thought.

People began screaming, bodies moving in frantic waves around me. No one knew where to run—where the shots were coming from or where safety might lie.

"We need to run!" Kevin appeared beside me, grabbing my arm. His face, illuminated by the distant lights of the Las Vegas Strip, was pale with fear.

We sprinted toward the vendor booths, stumbling over abandoned chairs and bags. The chaos was overwhelming—screams, gunfire, the pounding of feet. We ducked behind one of the booths, pressing our bodies against the thin wall as others crowded in with us.

The gunfire sounded closer now, more concentrated. A man beside me jolted, his body going rigid. A dark stain spread across his shirt.

Kevin kicked at the wall between the booth and a trailer, creating an opening. "Get up and run!" he shouted to our group, turning to the man beside me. "Run!"

The man's eyes stared upward, unseeing.

My feet moved before my mind could process what I'd seen. Kevin pulled me through the opening, and we were running again.

Outside, disorder ruled. Bodies pushed and shoved in every direction. A woman running beside me crumpled to the ground. I reached for her, but Kevin's grip on my wrist was firm, pulling me forward. I glanced back, unable to tell if she'd been shot or simply fallen in the crowd. The gunshots continued relentlessly.

Somehow, we found ourselves running toward the Tropicana.

A backstage wall opened before us—whether by design or accident, I couldn't tell. We ran through, uncertain if we were heading into danger or away from it.

A security guard stood at an exit, calmly directing people.

"Do you not know what's going on?" I screamed at him, my throat raw. "There's a shooting!"

His smile faltered, confusion replacing it.

We burst into the back entrance of the Tropicana's convention center, joining hundreds of other refugees from the festival. Strangers embraced me, weeping. I looked down at my arms, seeing thick droplets of blood spattered across my skin and clothes. Was I shot? I patted myself frantically before realizing—it wasn't my blood.

A new wave of screams erupted from the entrance. "Gunman! He's coming this way!" People began running again, a fresh surge of panic spreading like wildfire.

Kevin grabbed my hand and we ran for the elevators. Bodies pressed in around us as the doors closed. The elevator lurched upward, stopping at the eighth floor, refusing to go further with its overloaded cabin. Without hesitation, we poured out and ran for the stairs. Five flights up to the 13th floor—though the hotel called it the 14th. My bare feet hit against the concrete steps; I'd lost both shoes in the desperate escape.

I pounded on our hotel room door, gasping for breath. Lauren opened it, her annoyed expression quickly shifting to concern.

"What happened?" she asked, stepping back to let us in.

Kevin tried to explain between ragged breaths. Lauren's husband, Chris, tensed as she mentioned friends still at the concert. Before I could process what was happening, Kevin and Chris were heading back out, determined to help others.

"Don't go!" I pleaded, grabbing Kevin's arm. "We don't know if there are bombs or multiple shooters!"

But he was already moving, adrenaline driving him forward.

My stomach heaved. I barely made it to the bathroom before vomiting. When there was nothing left, I stumbled into the shower, watching as crimson water circled down the drain.

Blood—someone else's blood—washing from my body.

What happened? The question echoed in my mind, unanswerable.

~

Kevin returned safely, still shell-shocked. Lauren called my parents because my hands were shaking too badly to hold the phone.

My father called back moments later. "Oh, were you two in a gangster fight?" he joked, unaware of the magnitude of what had occurred.

"No," I whispered. "I think it was bigger than that."

We didn't sleep. Instead, we huddled together on the bed, refreshing news sites for information. *Three dead in Vegas shooting,* the first headline read.

Relief washed over me momentarily. "Oh, thank God, it wasn't as bad as I thought."

But with each refresh, the numbers climbed: five, nine, 13, 21, 36, 42....Finally, mercifully, the count stopped at 58 people dead.

At 5 am, we left our room. In the casino, people lay wrapped in sheets on the floor, unable to return to their own hotels. The drive back to Southern California passed in weighted silence, broken only when I answered my father's call. His sobs matched my own as the reality of what we'd survived finally hit us.

~

I later learned that 64-year-old Stephen Paddock had opened fire on us from his 32nd-floor suites in the Mandalay Bay hotel—the very hotel in which we'd initially planned to stay. He fired more than 1000 rounds, killing 60 people and wounding an estimated 867. The incident became the deadliest mass shooting in US history, with the shooter's motivation remaining unknown.

In the months that followed, I moved through life in a fog. Simple sounds—a car backfiring, a crowd of people gathered, even a balloon popping at an office party—would send me spiraling back into the dark heart of that night. My heart would race. My mind would freeze, caught between fight and flight.

Work became both a refuge and a challenge. I'd sit in meetings, nodding along while my thoughts scattered like birds at the sound of a gunshot. I wondered how many others around the office carried hidden traumas of their own. How many struggled to focus while battling memories that ambushed them without warning?

The question that kept returning wasn't why this happened, but what now? What could I do with this experience that might help others?

The answer emerged gradually. As a high-level executive, I realized I had an opportunity—perhaps even a responsibility—to transform my personal trauma into professional purpose. I began researching how trauma affects workplace performance, how it disrupts concentration, innovation and collaboration. I discovered organizations often lack frameworks for psychological safety after traumatic events.

It's hard to understand why not. For those who have not deeply considered trauma, it can seem diffuse and mysterious. From mass violence to personal loss, from natural disasters to health crises, trauma has many causes and takes many forms. But they all have a few aspects in common.

Using my own experience as a laboratory of sorts, I was able to develop frameworks in my own organization, refining approaches to supporting employees through various types of trauma—from mass violence to personal loss, from natural disasters to health crises.

With this book, I have distilled the best of what worked into actionable strategies you can apply in any sort of organization. It's not merely an explanation defining trauma in the workplace—it's a survival guide written from the trenches. Within these pages, you'll find practical tools for creating physically and psychologically safe environments where employees can process trauma without sacrificing their professional standing.

Whether you're a CEO, manager, human resources professional or in any other position of leadership, you'll discover how to recognize trauma responses that masquerade as performance issues. You'll learn concrete steps for rebuilding trust after organizational trauma. And you'll gain frameworks for crisis response that address both immediate safety needs and long-term psychological recovery. Each chapter closes with key takeaways you can begin to put into practice immediately.

Specifically, this book will equip you to:

- Understand trauma's biological and psychological dimensions—how it rewires neural pathways and disrupts cognitive function in ways unique to each individual's experience and background.
- Implement practical workplace interventions that acknowledge trauma without pathologizing employees or compromising organizational objectives.
- Develop comprehensive safety protocols that address not just physical threats but the complex aftermath of crisis events, including clear communication channels and leadership response frameworks.
- Apply the mentoring strategies I've developed to help teams move beyond limiting thought patterns that trauma often leaves in its wake—the fear-based decision-making, risk aversion and hypervigilance that can stall careers.
- Harness the transformative power of community in healing—creating structured support networks within your organization

that turn collective trauma into collective resilience.

My road from that night in Las Vegas to the insights in this book wasn't short, straight or easy. But it led to a proven framework that can be used to improve employee well-being, reduce trauma-related turnover and cultivate environments where people feel genuinely safe—not just physically protected, but psychologically supported. This isn't just about crisis management. It's about creating workplaces where trauma survivors don't just survive—they thrive, build and succeed.

1

WHEN CRISIS BECOMES OPPORTUNITY

My *experience was nothing like yours.*
When people learn I survived the Route 91 shooting, something shifts in their posture. Their shoulders drop slightly. Their voices soften to that careful tone reserved for handling fragile things. Then comes the retreat—not physical, but emotional. They start backing away from their own pain, dismissing their struggles with phrases that have become as predictable as they are heartbreaking.

I know it could be worse.

At least I wasn't there.

It doesn't compare to what you went through.

I watch it happen in their eyes—that instantaneous calculus where they measure their suffering against mine and find it wanting. As if trauma operates on some cosmic scoreboard. As if pain needs to come with headlines and body counts to earn validation. As if their shattered marriage, their father's slow death from cancer, their brutal layoff after 20 years of loyalty somehow shrinks to nothing beside the horror of that October night in Las Vegas.

Let me be absolutely clear: It doesn't work that way.

This belief—that only the most vivid and extreme stories count, that suffering requires a certain magnitude to matter—isn't just wrong. It's actively dangerous. It's how pain goes unacknowledged in boardrooms and break rooms alike. It's how people learn to swallow their anguish, to perform normalcy while something vital inside them slowly bleeds out. It's how organizations lose their humanity one buried trauma at a time.

If you're a leader—whether you manage two people or 2000—this understanding forms your foundation. Before you draft policies or design programs, before you implement strategies or measure outcomes, you must grasp this fundamental truth: All trauma matters. Every version of human suffering deserves recognition, space and response.

The statistics support this reality with sobering clarity. According to the World Health Organization, approximately 70 percent of people will experience trauma at some point in their lives.[1] That's not a possibility you can plan around or hope to avoid. That's a near-certainty sitting in your next staff meeting, walking your hallways, contributing to your bottom line. In your organization, that percentage translates to a simple fact: Most of the people around you are carrying far more than deadlines and performance metrics. They're shouldering loss, betrayal, abandonment, violence—some version of personal devastation that shapes every decision they make.

And they're doing it quietly, professionally and often invisibly.

Trauma refuses to fit neat categories. It doesn't announce itself with obvious symptoms or convenient timelines. It doesn't always manifest as tears streaming down faces during presentations or panic attacks in conference rooms. Sometimes trauma looks like the project manager who suddenly can't make decisions. The sales director who snaps at colleagues over minor issues. The administrative assistant who starts missing meetings after years of perfect attendance. The executive who becomes emotionally unreachable, conducting business from behind an invisible wall.

These behaviors aren't character flaws or "performance issues"—they're adaptive responses to experiences that overwhelmed the human capacity to cope. And those experiences come in forms as varied as the people who endure them.

Understanding the landscape of trauma begins with recognizing its three primary types, each leaving distinct imprints on behavior, cognition and workplace functioning.

Acute trauma strikes like a lightning bolt, splitting life into clear before and after segments. One moment, existence follows familiar patterns. Then, reality fractures into something unrecognizable. I experienced this transformation when gunfire erupted at the Route 91 Harvest country music festival. Between one heartbeat and the next, I shifted from dancing to a country song to running for my life through chaos I couldn't have imagined minutes earlier.

Your employees carry similar watersheds. The phone call announcing a spouse's sudden death. The car accident that changed everything in the space between green light and impact. The medical diagnosis that redefined every future plan. These events burn themselves into memory with terrifying precision, creating reference points that divide all subsequent experience into "before it happened" and "after everything changed."

Chronic trauma operates differently, building like sediment deposited by a slow-moving river. It doesn't announce itself with explosive moments but accumulates through prolonged exposure to harm or stress. This includes the employee enduring domestic violence who shows up each morning with carefully applied concealer hiding more than dark circles. The worker facing relentless harassment who begins avoiding team gatherings and collaborative projects. The manager who is trapped in a toxic organizational culture where psychological safety erodes through a thousand small cuts rather than one devastating blow. Because chronic trauma develops gradually, it often gets misdiagnosed as burnout, moodiness or simple disengagement. Leaders miss the deeper currents running beneath surface behaviors, attributing declining performance to attitude problems rather than recognizing the signs of a nervous system under siege.

Complex trauma cuts deepest of all, formed through repeated violations of trust and safety, often beginning in childhood and extending into adult relationships and institutions. This includes growing up in homes where love came with conditions of silence, surviving cycles of violence that created hypervigilance as a survival skill, enduring systemic neglect by the very organizations that promised security and growth.

Complex trauma doesn't just hurt—it rewires fundamental assumptions about safety, trust and human relationships. Employees carrying this burden may struggle with authority figures, withdraw from team-building exercises or react with surprising intensity to what others perceive as minor workplace conflicts. These responses aren't overblown or inappropriate—they're logical adaptations to a world that taught harsh lessons about power, reliability and emotional safety.

Understanding these distinctions matters because each type of trauma creates different challenges in workplace settings. But what unites all forms of traumatic experience is their profound impact on brain function—changes that directly affect the very skills most valued in professional environments.

When someone encounters overwhelming threat or stress, their brain's architecture shifts in ways that prioritize survival over everything else. The prefrontal cortex—the sophisticated command center responsible for logical reasoning, strategic planning, creative problem-solving and executive decision-making—essentially goes offline. In its place, the amygdala, that ancient alarm system designed to detect and respond to danger, takes operational control.[2]

This neurological shift isn't a character defect or sign of weakness. It's biology performing exactly as designed under extreme conditions. The brain narrows its focus to one essential question: *Am I safe right now?* Everything else—quarterly reports, project deadlines, team dynamics, career advancement—becomes secondary to that fundamental survival assessment.

This understanding reframes workplace behaviors that might otherwise seem puzzling or frustrating. When a previously decisive employee suddenly struggles to choose between viable options, they're not being indecisive—their brain's decision-making apparatus is operating under the influence of a hyperactive threat-detection system. When someone who typically handles stress well begins avoiding challenging assignments, they're not becoming lazy—they're responding to internal warning signals that have recalibrated their risk assessment mechanisms.

As a leader, recognizing this biological reality changes your entire approach to human performance challenges. It allows you to stop taking trauma responses personally, to move beyond frustration at behaviors that seem inexplicable and to start responding with both strategic thinking and genuine compassion.

Your role in these situations isn't to diagnose psychological conditions or provide therapeutic interventions. You're not qualified to fix your employees' trauma, nor should you attempt to do so. But you are uniquely positioned to create organizational conditions where traumatized nervous systems can begin to recalibrate, where people can access their full cognitive capabilities and where healing becomes possible alongside productivity.

This work starts with a fundamental shift in perspective—moving from judgment to curiosity, from frustration to understanding, from dismissal to recognition. It begins with the revolutionary act of taking all suffering seriously, regardless of its scale or source.

Because here's what I've learned in the years since that night in Las Vegas: Trauma doesn't compete. Pain doesn't require ranking. Your broken heart doesn't become less significant because someone else's world exploded in a different way. The grief you carry from your father's death doesn't shrink because someone else lost their child. The anxiety that grips you after a brutal restructuring doesn't disappear because others have faced worse betrayals.

Every wound deserves witness. Every struggle merits support. Every person carrying invisible burdens deserves leaders who understand that healing happens not through comparison, but through compassion.

Never underestimate someone else's pain just because it doesn't look like your own. And never let anyone—including yourself—minimize suffering just because worse things have happened to other people.

In the end, that's where real leadership begins: in the radical act of seeing all trauma as valid, all pain as deserving of response and all healing as worth supporting.

∾

UNDERSTANDING the concept of fight or flight becomes critically important when managing teams.[3] This acute stress response refers to physiological reactions triggered when someone encounters mentally or physically terrifying situations. Hormones flood the system, preparing the body to either confront the threat or escape to safety.

But fight or flight tells only half the story. Four

distinct responses emerge during trauma, each creating different workplace behaviors you must recognize:

The Four Faces of Survival

When the human nervous system detects a threat, it doesn't pause to analyze or strategize. It doesn't consider professional consequences or workplace appropriateness. It activates one of four hardwired survival responses, each designed by millions of years of evolution to keep us alive when danger strikes.[4] Understanding these responses—fight, flight, freeze and fawn—transforms how you interpret behaviors that might otherwise seem puzzling, problematic or even insubordinate.

Fight: When Defense Becomes Offense

Fight manifests as confrontation, aggression and pushback. It's the nervous system's attempt to eliminate perceived threats through force or intimidation. An employee operating from fight mode doesn't consciously choose aggression—their brain has determined that attack offers the best chance of survival.

Imagine Sarah, a marketing director who survived an abusive marriage before joining your company. During a routine budget meeting, when the CFO questions her department's spending with a sharp tone and imposing posture that unconsciously reminds her of her ex-husband's intimidation tactics, something shifts behind her eyes. Her jaw tightens. Her voice rises. She interrupts him mid-sentence, her words cutting like glass: "Don't you dare question my competence. I've delivered results every quarter while your accounting errors cost us thousands."

The room falls silent. Everyone stares. Sarah's face flushes as she realizes what just happened, but the damage spreads like ink in water. Later, colleagues whisper about her "attitude problem" and "inability to handle feedback." They don't see the invisible tripwire that was crossed, the way certain tones and gestures transported her nervous system back to a kitchen where raised voices preceded violence.

Or consider Marcus, whose childhood taught him that showing weakness invited punishment. During performance reviews, when managers offer constructive criticism, his body language shifts into combat readiness. His shoulders square, his voice drops to a dangerous quiet, and his responses become sharp-edged challenges rather than collaborative discussions. "I disagree with that assessment entirely," he states, eyes hard as stone. "Show me the data that supports your position." What appears as arrogance or defensiveness is actually a survival mechanism learned in a household where criticism was the prelude to humiliation.

Fight responses often puzzle managers because they seem disproportionate to workplace triggers. The employee who explodes over a scheduling change, the team member who turns minor feedback into a heated argument, the colleague who treats every meeting like a battlefield—they're not being difficult. They're responding to threats that exist more in their nervous system's memory than in the current moment's reality.

Flight: When Escape Becomes Strategy

Flight appears as avoidance, absenteeism and seeking escape. When the brain determines that confrontation is futile, it chooses distance as protection. These employees might physically leave situations or mentally check out, but their nervous system's message remains consistent: *Safety lies in being somewhere else.*

Watch Jennifer, who experienced workplace sexual harassment at her previous job. Now, when the monthly all-hands meetings are scheduled, her stomach begins churning days in advance. She calls in sick more frequently during weeks with large gatherings, claiming migraines that are real but rooted in anxiety rather than physical causes. When she does attend, she chooses seats near exits, checks her phone obsessively and seems to exist in a separate dimension from the discussion swirling around her.

Her manager notices the pattern but interprets it incorrectly. "Jennifer seems disengaged lately," he mentions to HR. "She's not participating in team events, and her attendance has become unreliable." What he can't see is how Jennifer's nervous system has, without consulting Jennifer, categorized large meetings as potential danger zones, places where predators might emerge from positions of authority. Her brain offers a simple solution: avoid the meetings, avoid the risk.

Flight can also manifest as workaholism when the workplace itself feels safer than other environments. Adam, whose home life is crumbling under the dark weight of his wife's addiction and unpredictable rages, begins arriving at the office earlier and staying later. He volunteers for every business trip, every weekend project and every other opportunity to be anywhere but where chaos waits for him. His desk becomes a fortress, his computer screen a portal to control and predictability that his personal life seems to lack entirely.

To colleagues, Adam appears dedicated, possibly overworked. To his manager, he seems like employee-of-the-year material. But his nervous system has simply identified the office as a refuge, and flight toward work becomes his primary coping mechanism. The irony goes unnoticed: His workplace performance improves while his overall well-being deteriorates, creating an unsustainable cycle that will eventually collapse.

Freeze: When Stillness Becomes Survival

Freeze describes the nervous system's most primitive response—the body's complete inability to move when facing perceived danger. If someone is frozen with fear, they cannot think clearly, move decisively or access their normal problem-solving abilities. In the workplace, this manifests as missed deadlines, paralysis when facing decisions and complete inability to function when challenges arise.

Imagine Rebecca, who witnessed a violent car accident that killed three people. The experience imprinted itself so deeply that unexpected loud sounds—even office construction or enthusiastic applause—trigger an immediate freeze response. During the quarterly presentation where she's supposed to announce her team's achievements, the sudden sound of the microphone feeding back sends her nervous system into lockdown. She stands at the podium, mouth open but no words emerging, eyes wide but unfocused, body rigid as marble.

Minutes pass. The audience shifts uncomfortably. Her manager prompts her twice before she snaps back to awareness, stammering through an abbreviated version of her prepared remarks. Later, colleagues describe her as "not ready for leadership" or "cracking under pressure." They don't understand that her brain momentarily transported her to that intersection where twisted metal and screaming sirens taught her that sudden sounds meant death was nearby.

Freeze responses can be subtler but equally paralyzing. Thomas, whose father's explosive anger terrorized his childhood home, finds himself unable to make decisions when his current supervisor displays any signs of irritation. During project planning meetings, when deadlines grow tight and voices become slightly raised, Thomas's cognitive abilities simply vanish. He sits motionless, staring at his laptop screen, unable to process the information being discussed or contribute meaningfully to solutions.

His manager interprets this as disinterest or incompetence. "Thomas just shuts down when things get challenging," she tells HR. "I'm not sure he's cut out for this role." But Thomas's brain has categorized raised voices and time pressure as danger signals, and his nervous system responds by essentially pressing the pause button on all nonessential functions—including the executive reasoning skills his job requires.

The cruelest aspect of freeze responses is how they mimic laziness or indifference to outside observers. The employee who can't complete simple tasks after witnessing a workplace accident, the manager who becomes paralyzed by decisions after experiencing a personal trauma, the team member whose productivity plummets following a frightening incident—they're often labeled as problems rather than people whose nervous systems are struggling to recalibrate.

Fawn: When Pleasing Becomes Survival

Fawn describes desperate attempts to appease perceived threats—a response most commonly seen in those who experienced chronic trauma, particularly in childhood or relationships where survival depended on keeping dangerous people happy. This response teaches the nervous system that safety comes through submission, compliance and making oneself indispensable to potential aggressors.

Consider Christina, whose childhood was spent navigating an alcoholic father's unpredictable moods. She learned that paying attention to his slightest changes in tone, anticipating his needs before he expressed them and absorbing his anger without resistance kept the household relatively peaceful. Now, at 35, she brings those same survival skills to her corporate environment, where they manifest as extreme people-pleasing that borders on self-destruction.

When her supervisor mentions being stressed about an upcoming deadline, Christina immediately volunteers to stay late every night for two weeks, despite having her own family obligations. When colleagues complain about their workloads, she quietly absorbs their tasks without being asked, working through lunch breaks and weekends to ensure no one experiences frustration that might be directed toward her. She agrees to impossible timelines, accepts blame for others' mistakes and sacrifices her own professional development opportunities to make her manager's life easier.

To leadership, Christina appears to be the ideal employee—dedicated, selfless and reliable. Her performance reviews praise her "team-first attitude" and "willingness to go above and beyond." But her nervous system has categorized workplace harmony as essential to survival, and her reflexive fawn response drives her to exhaust herself in service of others' comfort. She becomes increasingly vulnerable to exploitation because her trauma history has wired her to believe that her own needs are negotiable while others' needs are matters of life and death.

The fawn response can also manifest as compulsive agreement and avoidance of conflict at all costs. Let's take Kevin, whose childhood home was a minefield of his mother's bipolar episodes and who learned that disagreeing with authority figures invited chaos. In workplace settings, he nods enthusiastically to every suggestion, supports contradictory viewpoints within the same meeting and never advocates for his own ideas or needs.

During an aggressive round of budget cuts, as his department faces layoffs, Kevin doesn't negotiate for his position or highlight his contributions. Instead, he volunteers to have his salary reduced, offers to shoulder additional responsibilities and suggests that others might be more deserving of job security. His manager appreciates his "mature attitude" about the situation, not realizing that Kevin's nervous system has interpreted the layoffs as confirmation that his survival depends on making himself as agreeable and unthreatening as possible—whatever it may cost Kevin and the rest of his team in the long run.

The Brain Under Pressure

These four responses create lasting neurological changes that affect every aspect of cognitive function. The amygdala—that ancient alarm system buried deep in the brain's emotional center—becomes hyperactive and hypersensitive after traumatic experiences. Like a smoke detector with a broken sensitivity setting, it begins interpreting ordinary workplace situations as five-alarm emergencies.

Brain imaging studies reveal the stark differences between traumatized and healthy brains. PTSD creates visible alterations in brain structure and function that show up clearly in scans—the amygdala enlarged and overactive like a swollen, infected alarm system that won't stop ringing. Meanwhile, the prefrontal cortex, that sophisticated command center responsible for logic, planning and executive function, shows decreased activity and connectivity.[5]

During traumatic events, the body floods itself with adrenaline, cortisol and other stress hormones designed for short-term survival. But when trauma becomes chronic or remains unresolved, these chemical messengers continue circulating at dangerous levels, literally rewiring neural pathways. The brain begins storing traumatic memories differently than normal experiences—not as coherent narratives with clear beginnings, middles and ends, but as fragmented sensory impressions embedded directly into the amygdala.

This creates a phenomenon where traumatic experiences don't feel like memories—they feel like present-moment reality. The smell of coffee might transport someone back to the break room where they received news of their child's death. The sound of a particular ringtone might trigger the fight response in someone whose abusive ex-husband used that same alert. The feeling of being watched during presentations might freeze someone whose trauma taught them that attention often preceded attack.

These sensory imprints bypass the brain's rational processing centers. They don't respond to logic or reassurance because they don't operate in the realm of conscious, rational thought. They operate at the level of pure survival instinct, where milliseconds matter more than social appropriateness and staying alive trumps every other consideration.

The result is employees whose nervous systems have been reprogrammed to interpret ordinary workplace interactions as potential threats. The quarterly review becomes an interrogation. The team meeting becomes an ambush. The supervisor's unexpected request for a private conversation becomes a sting operation. Their brains, scarred by experiences that taught harsh lessons about human nature and personal safety, scan every interaction for signs of impending danger.

Understanding this neurological reality transforms how leaders approach performance issues, behavioral problems and employee development challenges. The marketing director who explodes during budget discussions, the project manager who can't make decisions under pressure and the administrative assistant who agrees to impossible deadlines—they're not being difficult, incompetent or intentionally obtuse. They're responding to internal warning systems that have been calibrated by experiences most people never want to imagine.

This knowledge doesn't excuse problematic behavior or eliminate the need for professional standards. But it does provide a framework for responding with both strategic thinking and human compassion, creating possibilities for healing rather than further harm.

How Trauma Hierarchies Erode Trust

Not long after the shooting, a close friend experienced her own traumatic moment—her toddler began choking during a meal. She saw it happening but froze, struck rigid by fear and helplessness. Eventually, she managed to perform the Heimlich, and the food came loose. Her son was okay. But afterward, she couldn't shake the panic. For weeks, every mealtime became a ritual of silent pleading: *Please don't choke, please don't choke.*

When she told me her story, I felt no doubt her experience was traumatic. My trauma didn't make hers less real or valid—quite the contrary. Her fear was genuine, and as a mother, I could relate completely.

This distinction matters profoundly for leaders. No hierarchy of traumatic experiences exists for the resulting symptoms. Because I survived a mass shooting doesn't mean someone who experienced a smaller-scale trauma won't feel the exact same emotional intensity—or even more. Everyone's experience of trauma is unique, bringing different coping strategies and stress responses based on lived experiences, personality and biological makeup.

For leaders, this means never comparing employee experiences or dismissing someone's struggle because it seems "minor" compared to others. The moment you create a trauma hierarchy in your workplace, you destroy psychological safety and prevent employees from seeking the support they need.

When Personal History Becomes Professional Strength

Growing up with dyslexia taught me early that I would have to work harder than others to succeed. In third grade, while classmates breezed through reading exercises, I stumbled over simple words and watched the clock tick down as unanswered questions piled up. The diagnosis brought deep shame—I hated being different and struggling more than my peers.

During "popcorn reading"—when teachers randomly called on students to read aloud—I lived in terror. To avoid humiliation, I overprepared, taking reading work home and memorizing sentences word by word. When called on, I'd recall what was on the page without actually reading aloud. These chronic feelings of hypervigilance and shame were my first experiences with trauma.

I spent my childhood finding ways to appear smarter and overcompensate. I had extremely low self-esteem, thinking I was *bad* at most things. To overcome this, I learned to overcompensate—spending hours reviewing academic materials, training myself to memorize content since actually learning concepts was too difficult.

By high school, I knew how to hide my dyslexia. But this came at a cost. Years of hypervigilance and over-preparation were exhausting. Despite all my efforts, I earned C's at best. It became disheartening to do twice the work of classmates only to earn fewer points and lower grades.

Geometry class nearly prevented my graduation. Despite extra credit and hours of homework, I maintained only a D. Approaching my teacher in desperation, I essentially begged for help.

"I'm the only senior in this class and I know I need a C to graduate," I said, almost crying. "Is there anything I can do to bring my grade up?"

"Carly, I know you've worked hard," he said. "Keep doing what you've been doing. Turn in your work on time. It may just be enough to bring up your grade."

This became a turning point. Here was a leader who cared and gave me a chance because he recognized my effort. He saw that I was putting in more work than peers earning A's. This proved that effort *does* count, and that if you consistently show up and work hard, people notice. I got the C needed to pass.

I'll never know if he gave it to me or if I *earned* it. Either way, I graduated with a lifelong lesson that shaped my leadership philosophy: If you consistently show up and work hard, you can accomplish goals that once seemed out of reach.

While having dyslexia and feeling ashamed throughout childhood was traumatic, it also catalyzed my work ethic. This characteristic put me in situations a student who struggled to read might not usually find themselves in—hosting radio shows, managing teams and eventually leading organizations through crisis.

For leaders, my story illustrates a crucial principle: Trauma doesn't disqualify someone from success. With proper support, traumatic experiences can become sources of extraordinary resilience, empathy and leadership capability. The employee struggling with PTSD might become your most compassionate manager. The team member with childhood trauma might develop unparalleled skills in conflict resolution.

The Business Case for Trauma-Informed Leadership

One reason I was able to return to work after the shooting was that I had a supportive, understanding leader who took time to understand what I was experiencing. Not only did I feel supported, but I was also able to continue working while processing my PTSD. Through that process, I observed countless ways thoughtful leaders can support those "processing on the go."

If you lead an organization, you can be certain that someone working with you has experienced trauma. It might be death of a loved one, car accident, assault, witnessing violence, sexual assault or harassment. It's not a matter of *if* an employee will experience trauma but *when*.

The business and human costs of neglecting this reality are devastating: higher turnover, increased conflict, decreased productivity and low staff morale. When employees feel unsupported during their most vulnerable moments, they leave—taking their institutional knowledge, relationships and potential with them. Replacing a single employee costs between 50–

200 percent of their annual salary, depending on the role.[6]

The mathematics are stark, but they tell part of the story. For every employee who walks out the door carrying unhealed wounds, there's an untold narrative of what could have been—the innovations never shared, the mentoring relationships never formed and the loyalty never earned. These losses compound invisibly, creating organizational deficits that show up in quarterly reports as unexplained dips in performance, mysterious increases in sick days and the kind of cultural malaise that executives struggle to diagnose. But here's what traditional cost-benefit analyses miss: the same investment that prevents these losses doesn't just stop the bleeding—it transforms the entire equation.

While some leaders worry that acknowledging trauma will open floodgates of dysfunction or create cultures of victimhood, the opposite often proves true. Organizations that embrace trauma-informed leadership don't just do the right thing—they achieve measurable competitive advantages that directly impact their bottom line. The data tells a compelling story, but the human stories behind that data reveal why trauma-informed leadership has become the secret weapon of industry leaders.

Increased Retention: When Support Creates Loyalty

Employees who feel genuinely supported during a crisis don't just stay—they develop the kind of fierce loyalty that money can't buy. This isn't sentimentality; it's a strategic advantage disguised as human decency.

Consider what might happen when an account manager's husband receives a terminal cancer diagnosis. Instead of the typical "take what time you need" platitudes followed by subtle pressure to maintain productivity, trauma-informed leaders implement what one CEO calls "crisis protocols."

The employee's workload gets redistributed without fanfare. Direct reports receive temporary mentoring from senior staff. Most importantly, the position remains secure with full benefits while she navigates months of hospital visits, treatment decisions and end-of-life planning.

When she returns to work after her husband's death, she brings something unexpected: a level of commitment that transforms her entire department. She begins staying late not because she has to, but because she wants to. She mentors struggling colleagues with patience that seems limitless. When competitors try recruiting her with substantial salary increases, she declines without hesitation. "They supported me when my world collapsed," she tells friends. "I'm not going anywhere."

Years later, she leads the company's largest accounts and has personally prevented multiple key employees from leaving for competitors. Her retention alone saves hundreds of thousands in recruitment and training costs, while her increased performance generates millions in additional revenue.

This pattern repeats across trauma-informed organizations. At one software company, when a developer disclosed his struggle with PTSD following a car accident, managers didn't just offer employee assistance program resources. They redesigned his workspace to reduce triggers, allowed flexible scheduling for therapy appointments and paired him with a peer mentor who had navigated similar challenges. His productivity actually increased after receiving support, and he became an informal ambassador for the company's culture, referring multiple high-caliber candidates who specifically chose the organization because of its reputation for supporting employees through difficulties.

The mathematics of retention becomes even more compelling when organizations calculate the true cost of turnover. Beyond recruitment expenses, companies lose institutional knowledge, client relationships and team cohesion every time traumatized employees leave because they feel unsupported. Trauma-informed organizations flip this equation, turning potential departures into demonstrations of loyalty that create recruiting advantages.

Enhanced Productivity: The Psychology of Peak Performance

When people feel psychologically safe, they don't just work harder—they work smarter, take better-calculated risks and contribute ideas and innovations that drive organizational growth. Trauma-informed workplaces create conditions where human potential flourishes rather than merely survives.

Imagine a managing director at a consulting firm, who, one day, not long after implementing trauma-informed leadership training for all managers, noticed something remarkable. Team productivity didn't just improve gradually—it surged within months. Projects that previously took teams six weeks to complete were finished in four, often under budget. Client satisfaction scores increased by nearly a quarter. Most telling, employees began volunteering for challenging assignments they would have avoided under previous leadership approaches.

The transformation wasn't mysterious. Imagine an associate consultant who, one day, felt comfortable disclosing her anxiety disorder and received accommodations like written follow-ups to verbal instructions and advance notice of presentation requirements. Her performance skyrocketed. She stopped spending mental energy managing her symptoms in secret and redirected that cognitive capacity toward client work.

Her billable hour quality improved so dramatically that clients began requesting her specifically for complex projects.

This psychological safety effect compounds across teams. When employees witness colleagues receiving support rather than punishment for struggling, they become more willing to admit mistakes early, ask for help before problems escalate and share innovative ideas that might initially seem risky. The result is organizations that adapt faster, innovate more frequently and solve problems more creatively than competitors operating under fear-based management.

Research supports these observations with hard numbers. Teams with high psychological safety show 19 percent higher accuracy on routine tasks, 27 percent reduction in turnover and 76 percent more engagement compared to teams where employees fear negative consequences for vulnerability.[7] For trauma-informed organizations, these statistics translate into competitive advantages that compound over time.

Improved Recruitment: Reputation as a Strategic Asset

Organizations known for supporting employees during difficult times don't just attract more candidates—they attract top talent who actively choose them over competitors offering higher salaries or better perks. In an era where professionals research company culture as thoroughly as compensation packages, trauma-informed reputations become powerful differentiators.

Imagine a tech startup that learned this lesson painfully when it lost three consecutive finalist candidates to competitors. Exit interviews revealed a disturbing pattern: Candidates were researching company reviews and social media presence, thereby finding stories about how previous employees were treated during personal crises. One finalist specifically mentioned choosing a competitor because "I want to work somewhere that treats people like humans, not just resources." Ouch!

The CEO leaped into action, implementing comprehensive trauma-informed policies, but more importantly, sharing stories about how the company supported employees through difficulties. When a senior developer publicly thanked the company for accommodating his needs during his mother's battle with Alzheimer's, that social media post generated more high-quality job applications than any traditional recruiting campaign yet tried.

Within 18 months, the company's hiring pipeline transformed completely. Instead of struggling to attract talent, it began receiving unsolicited applications from experienced professionals specifically drawn to its supportive culture. The quality of candidates improved dramatically as word spread through professional networks that this was "a place that has your back when life gets complicated."

The recruiting advantage extends beyond individual applications. Trauma-informed organizations often find that their own employees become their most effective recruiters, actively encouraging former colleagues and industry connections to apply. When employees genuinely believe their workplace will support them through life's inevitable challenges, they stake their professional reputations on recommending friends and colleagues.

This organic recruiting network becomes particularly valuable in competitive industries where top talent has no shortage of options. Companies competing solely on salary and benefits find themselves outmaneuvered by organizations offering something more valuable: genuine security that extends beyond job functions to human dignity.

Reduced Legal Risk: Prevention as Protection

Trauma-informed policies don't just create better workplaces—they provide robust legal protection against discrimination claims, hostile workplace lawsuits and regulatory violations. By proactively addressing trauma responses, organizations prevent many situations that typically escalate into expensive legal battles.

Think of a law firm that discovered this protection

value when its charismatic office manager began displaying concerning behaviors after her divorce—missed deadlines, emotional outbursts during meetings and conflicts with colleagues. Under traditional management approaches, she would likely have faced progressive discipline leading to termination and potential wrongful dismissal claims.

Instead, the managing partner recognized potential trauma responses and initiated supportive interventions. She received temporary schedule modifications, plus access to counseling resources and mentoring support. Within three months, her performance returned to previous levels. More importantly, the firm avoided what could have been a costly legal battle, as her divorce involved domestic violence that could have supported discrimination and failure-to-accommodate claims.

This proactive approach creates documentation that demonstrates good-faith efforts to support struggling employees rather than punish them. When organizations can show they attempted reasonable accommodations and provided appropriate resources, they significantly strengthen their legal positions in any disputes that do arise.

Trauma-informed policies also reduce the likelihood of harassment and discrimination complaints by creating cultures where problematic behaviors are addressed early, decisively and supportively. Employees who feel heard and supported are less likely to resort to external legal remedies, while clear policies provide frameworks for addressing concerning behaviors before they escalate into violations.

Stronger Company Culture: The Compound Effect of Mutual Support

Teams that support each other through adversity develop bonds that transcend typical workplace relationships. This cultural strength becomes particularly valuable during organizational challenges, market downturns and competitive pressures when companies need employees to go beyond job descriptions.

Imagine a manufacturing company that experienced this cultural resilience when a long-term employee was diagnosed with cancer requiring extensive treatment. Instead of simply offering medical leave, the entire production team reorganized to cover his responsibilities while maintaining its own productivity levels. Supervisors provided flexible scheduling for anyone wanting to visit him during treatment. The company organized meal trains for his family and fundraising drives for medical expenses.

When he returned to work months later, he found a team transformed by shared purpose. Productivity had actually increased during his absence as employees collaborated more effectively than ever before. Interdepartmental conflicts that had simmered for months disappeared as people who had worked together to support their colleague continued applying that same collaborative spirit to daily challenges.

The cultural impact extended far beyond his situation. When the company faced its largest order in company history months later, requiring overtime and weekend work, employees volunteered enthusiastically. They had learned that supporting each other benefited everyone, and they trusted leadership to recognize their extra efforts during future personal challenges.

This mutual support culture creates organizational resilience that competitors struggle to replicate. When employees genuinely care about each other's well-being, they work harder to prevent colleagues from being overwhelmed, share knowledge more freely and maintain morale during difficult periods. The result is organizations that weather storms more effectively and emerge stronger from challenges that might cripple less cohesive competitors.

The Strategic Imperative

These benefits aren't accidental byproducts of being nice—they're predictable outcomes of creating psychological safety where human potential can flourish. Trauma-informed leadership doesn't require sacrificing performance standards or overlooking accountability.

Instead, it recognizes that supporting people through their struggles often unlocks capabilities that fear-based management keeps buried.

From what I've seen, organizations implementing trauma-informed approaches often report that their biggest surprise isn't the human benefits—it's the business results. When people feel genuinely supported, they don't take advantage of that support; they honor it through increased dedication, innovation and loyalty.

In an economy where talent retention, productivity and cultural strength determine competitive advantage, trauma-informed leadership has evolved from a moral imperative to a business necessity. The question isn't whether organizations can afford to implement these approaches—it's whether they can afford not to.

The business case is clear, but understanding the need for action and knowing how to act are two different challenges entirely. Many leaders find themselves caught between recognition and paralysis—they see the evidence, accept the logic, yet hesitate at the threshold of implementation. The hesitation is understandable: Trauma feels clinical, complex and outside the traditional scope of management training. But here's the truth that cuts through that complexity: You don't need a psychology degree to create psychological safety. You don't need to become a therapist to become a trauma-informed leader.

· · ·

WHILE IT'S NOT your responsibility to directly treat an employee's trauma—without the proper training, it would be irresponsible to try—it *is* your responsibility to offer appropriate support. Leadership must understand that the time to act is *now*. You can start by truly understanding trauma, its impact on the brain and the lasting effects it creates.

When you act now, you create a workplace where people don't just survive difficult experiences—they thrive because of the support they receive. This transforms your organization into a place people want to work, helping retain current employees and attract dedicated individuals motivated to contribute to something meaningful.

Post-traumatic stress disorder (PTSD) affects an estimated 13 million Americans as of 2020, manifesting through four primary categories: intrusion symptoms (unwanted thoughts, nightmares, flashbacks), avoidance behaviors (withdrawing from triggering activities or people), mood changes (depression, inability to feel joy, loss of interest in previously enjoyed activities) and reactivity changes (irritability, anger, sleep difficulties, hypervigilance).[9]

Without treatment, PTSD is unlikely to disappear on its own, no matter how much time you give it. Daily workplace interactions can trigger memories of trauma, causing intense emotional and physical reactions. Fortunately, many treatment options exist—including trauma-focused psychotherapy, cognitive behavioral therapy and holistic approaches like mindfulness and art therapy—that can help people not only cope with PTSD but heal completely.

For leaders, understanding PTSD symptoms helps distinguish between performance issues and trauma responses. The employee who suddenly can't concentrate in meetings might be experiencing intrusion symptoms. The team member avoiding group projects might be in avoidance mode. The colleague who seems perpetually on edge might be struggling with reactivity changes.

This knowledge transforms your leadership approach from reactive discipline to proactive support, creating environments where healing becomes possible alongside productivity.

∿

Key Takeaways

Trauma is inevitable in your workforce: Seventy percent of people globally experience trauma; plan for this reality rather than hoping to avoid it.

Four stress responses affect workplace performance: Fight, flight, freeze and fawn responses create different behavioral patterns you must recognize and respond to appropriately.

Brain changes from trauma are biological, not

character flaws: Understanding that post-trauma struggles reflect neurological changes, not weakness, prevents harmful misconceptions and enables compassionate leadership.

No trauma hierarchy exists: The intensity of an employee's response doesn't correlate to the severity of their experience; every person's trauma deserves validation and support.

Early intervention prevents costly outcomes: Addressing trauma support proactively reduces turnover, maintains productivity and enhances your organization's reputation as an employer of choice.

Support doesn't mean treatment: Your role is creating supportive environments and connecting employees with appropriate resources, not providing therapy.

Recovery enhances performance: Trauma-informed leadership can facilitate healing and even post-traumatic growth, transforming struggling employees into your strongest team members.

2

BEYOND THE BREAK: SUPPORTING TRAUMATIZED EMPLOYEES

Before we explore the frameworks and strategies that transform workplaces, it is important to grasp something fundamental. Safety isn't just about policies and procedures. It's about the invisible architecture of trust that either supports or undermines every interaction in your organization. This architecture gets built early—in the experiences that teach us whether the world is fundamentally safe or dangerous, whether people can be trusted or must be managed and whether vulnerability leads to support or exploitation.

Consider the difference between two employees facing the same workplace crisis. One approaches you directly when struggling, asks for help without shame and trusts that disclosure won't derail their career. The other suffers in silence, performs through pain and views any sign of struggle as a potential threat to their livelihood. The difference between them has nothing to do with character or competence—it's the foundation of safety they learned long before they walked into your building.

This foundation gets laid in childhood, in the earliest relationships that teach us what to expect from other people. It's reinforced through every subsequent experience with authority figures, institutions and communities. By the time employees enter your workplace, we carry invisible blueprints that determine how we might respond to stress, authority and vulnerability. Understanding these blueprints—and how they shape workplace behavior—is essential for any leader who wants to create genuinely supportive environments.

Some employees learned safety in homes that felt like fortresses against the world's chaos—places where bikes cluttered lawns and neighborhood kids gathered without fear, where parents showed up reliably and advocated fiercely when needed. Others learned vigilance in homes where love came with conditions, where survival required reading moods and managing others' emotions, where asking for help often invited more harm than healing.

Neither experience is right nor wrong, but both create lasting templates for how people navigate professional relationships. The employee who grew up with unconditional support brings different assumptions about workplace conflict than the one who learned that disagreement meant danger. The person whose parents modeled healthy problem-solving approaches challenges differently than someone whose childhood taught them that problems must be hidden to maintain relationships.

These early lessons about safety become particularly crucial during workplace trauma. When a crisis strikes—whether it's a personal emergency, organizational upheaval or broader catastrophe—people don't just respond to the current situation. They respond through the lens of every previous experience that taught them how dangerous the world might be and how trustworthy authority figures actually are.

The employee who learned that adults could be counted on to provide support during difficulties will approach you differently than the one whose experience taught them that revealing weakness invites abandonment. The person whose family modeled resilience through collaboration will handle team challenges differently than someone who learned that survival requires going it alone.

This isn't about judging anyone's background or making excuses for problematic behavior. It's about understanding the invisible influences that shape how people respond to your leadership, especially during their most vulnerable moments. When you recognize that every employee carries a unique foundation of safety—or lack thereof—you can begin creating environments that honor those differences while building new experiences of trustworthiness, allowing your team to thrive like never before.

The most effective trauma-informed leaders understand that they're not just managing current situations —they're either reinforcing old patterns of safety and trust, or they're creating opportunities for people to experience something different. Every interaction becomes a chance to demonstrate that this workplace doesn't operate by the same harmful rules.

This means recognizing that the confident project manager who suddenly can't make decisions might be responding not just to current stress, but to childhood lessons about what happens when you get things wrong. The team member who agrees to impossible deadlines might be operating from early programming that equated saying no with risking relationships. The employee who explodes over minor feedback might be responding to authority figures who taught them that criticism was the prelude to rejection.

Understanding these deeper patterns doesn't mean becoming a therapist for your team—some things are best left to professionals. But it does mean recognizing that creating psychological safety requires more than good intentions and company policies. It requires understanding how early experiences of safety and danger continue to influence adult behavior, especially during times of stress and vulnerability.

The foundation of safety your employees learned in their earliest relationships becomes the lens through which they interpret your leadership. When you understand this dynamic, you can begin building organizational cultures that either heal old wounds or, at a minimum, avoid replicating the patterns that created them.

In this chapter, we'll explore how these early foundations of safety shape adult behavior in professional settings. You'll learn to recognize the signs of different safety templates and understand how trauma can disrupt even the strongest foundations. Most importantly, you'll discover practical strategies for creating workplace experiences that build new patterns of trust and support, regardless of what your employees learned before they met you.

Because here's what every trauma-informed leader eventually discovers: You can't change your employees' histories, but you can absolutely influence their futures. The safety they experience in your organization becomes part of their foundation too—and that's a responsibility worth taking seriously.

When Strong Foundations Meet Unexpected Storms

From my first days, I felt a strong sense of safety. Growing up in a two-story house on a corner lot in Orange County, California, I knew what it felt like to have parents who showed up consistently, defended me when teachers weren't giving me deserved credit and created a social haven where neighborhood kids gathered because it felt like the safest place on the block. My dad never missed a soccer game or track meet. When I was on college radio, I'd come home to find him listening to my show, ready with positive feedback and unwavering support.

My mother's story taught me that resilience could be built even from difficult beginnings. As one of four children in a family without much money, she learned early to work hard and overcome difficulties without much support. She didn't attend college but was determined to succeed. After her father helped her get a job at Boeing, she eventually moved to Northrop Grumman, working on the stealth bomber and developing coding and troubleshooting skills despite battling an undiagnosed learning disability. She figured things out the hard way, often alone, until she built a successful career that became our family's financial foundation when my dad's car sales income proved unpredictable.

Watching her carry our family's financial burden when my dad was eventually laid off, I learned that hard work, determination and community support could overcome almost any obstacle. Both parents supported me completely—my dad advocating for me whenever needed, my mom modeling the kind of strength that turns challenges into stepping stones. Their consistent presence taught me that the world was fundamentally safe, that people could be trusted and that asking for help was not only acceptable, but essential.

This foundation served me well throughout my career. I became the dependable, independent employee who showed up and did her work no matter what. I approached challenges with confidence, trusted my supervisors and assumed that difficulty was temporary and manageable. My childhood had taught me that with enough support and effort, any problem could be solved.

But here's what leaders need to understand about trauma: It doesn't discriminate based on the strength of your foundation. It doesn't matter how safe your childhood was, how supportive your family remains or how resilient you've proven yourself to be. When trauma strikes, it creates cracks in even the most solid foundations—and those cracks can fundamentally alter how someone experiences safety, trust and vulnerability in professional settings.

After the Route 91 shooting, I took a week off work, needing time to process what happened and ensure I had a handle on life before jumping back into routine. No one I worked with had ever experienced something like this. While my boss, Aaron, wanted to be supportive, he wasn't sure what to do. Neither was I.

Up to this point, I had spent my life being the person others could count on—the reliable daughter who made her parents proud, the dedicated employee who never caused problems, the friend who held others up during their struggles. Even though Aaron told me to take the time I needed, I felt pressure to return as soon as possible. The thought of not being at work made me uneasy. However, the thought of going back made me nervous too.

When I finally returned, Aaron did his best to support me. At the time, our company had no official policies in place for employees returning to work post-trauma. We were still a very small company with an HR department of one. Looking back, I realize having something in place for trauma survivors returning to work would have been enormously helpful—not just for me, but for my boss too. Aaron wasn't prepared to deal with an employee who'd been in a mass shooting any more than I was prepared to return seamlessly to work. None of us had training or skills to handle this situation.

For leaders, this scenario represents both a critical vulnerability and a strategic opportunity. Helping employees transition back to work post-trauma is more than compassionate leadership—it's a business imperative that protects your most valuable assets. And it's particularly crucial to understand that trauma affects people regardless of their backgrounds, support systems or previous resilience. The marketing director who grew up in a loving home can be just as profoundly impacted by workplace trauma as the project manager whose childhood was marked by instability.

The Business Case for Return Protocols

Leaders should take trauma seriously for compelling financial and operational reasons. On the most basic level, having prepared responses to post-traumatic events removes the stress from leadership trying to improvise solutions during emotional crises. It provides clear paths for employees *and* management regarding expectations around time off, therapy appointments and handling the fact that employees may act differently when returning to work.

The best way to help staff return to work? Make it acceptable to be different.

I wasn't the same person after the event. When I returned to work, I was still thinking about the shooting constantly. I remember hearing a small explosion outside my office window.

Pop. Pop.

I could feel my chest tighten and my heart start pounding. I knew it wasn't shooting, but my body responded as though I were in a violent situation.

I had to talk to myself to stay calm.

Everything is okay, Carly. It's just a car outside. You are safe.

Despite growing up in a home where my parents had always been able to fix problems and make things better, I now carried experiences that couldn't be fixed or made better—only managed and integrated. The foundation of safety my parents had built for me remained solid, but trauma had added new layers that required different kinds of support.

On other days, while sitting at my desk, I found myself replaying the event, unable to focus. I would relive what happened over and over again, my mind transporting me back to that night while my colleagues continued their meetings around me.

For leaders, understanding these manifestations prevents costly misinterpretations. When an employee suddenly can't concentrate in meetings or seems jumpy around loud noises, you're witnessing neurobiological responses, not performance issues requiring disciplinary action.

My hypervigilance became my new normal. I wouldn't say I was naive before the shooting, but I don't remember thinking about exit strategies or crowd control as if my life depended on it. Growing up in a neighborhood where kids played freely in driveways and parents felt comfortable letting children roam, I had internalized a general sense of safety about the world. After the shooting, I was hyperaware of my surroundings, more sensitive to overly crowded places and constantly making exit plans and devising safety strategies.

When trauma survivors return to work, they're not just processing their experiences—they're fundamentally changed. Someone who was once laid-back and easygoing might now seem rigid and difficult. They might be hypervigilant, trying to predict every possible danger scenario. Someone might return to their office and realize it's nowhere near an exit, beginning to wonder how they might reach safety during a crisis.

These changes aren't temporary adjustments— they're lasting alterations in how people process their environment. Prepare for these shifts and remain flexible when possible, because the alternative is losing experienced employees who feel unsupported during their most vulnerable moments.

Creating Systematic Support Frameworks

To prepare for supporting employees post-trauma, delegate planning responsibility to someone with subject-matter expertise—ideally someone in HR with mental health training or crisis management experience. This person should develop comprehensive documentation that includes clearly defined employee rights.

This could include:

- Allocating time off for therapy appointments or doctor visits
- Ensuring the employee understands how to submit leave requests
- Going over what documentation is required for leave, appointments and things of that nature
- Making sure the employee understands what protections exist against retaliation for missed work or delayed productivity

Some employees may lack access to needed resources, and management should prepare to bridge those gaps. Employers can provide:

- Names of local or online mental health agencies specializing in trauma
- Information on PTSD symptoms and signs to watch for
- Relevant resources like crisis hotlines

It's not enough to provide phone numbers and check the "due diligence" box. Clear communication is key. Managers must assure staff they're open to listening and want to work together creating work environments that feel safe.

Leaders should go further by explicitly stating: *I want to know when you're struggling with your work.* If PTSD symptoms become so severe that someone cannot return to work, clarify steps to follow protocol. This proactive involvement deters employees from simply not showing up or quitting at the first sign of struggle—protecting both employee welfare and company investment.

Establish who employees need to speak with (human resources or an identified management staff member) and ensure employees trust that person. Reassure staff they will not be fired or reprimanded for discussing their needs. By developing this plan proactively, employees feel supported and managers can feel confident their teams will continue functioning.

Research consistently shows that employees who don't feel supported at work will not return, resulting in lost profit and productivity for companies—not to mention human cost. The investment in systematic support frameworks pays dividends in retention, morale and operational stability.

Next, managers and workers should discuss how to handle situations or colleagues that may be triggering. This might involve moving workstations closer to exits, setting boundaries with co-workers asking invasive

questions or adjusting meeting formats to accommodate concentration difficulties.

Leadership should also understand disability policies, including short-term disability coverage that typically pays 40 to 70 percent of base salary for non-work-
related conditions preventing work for set periods.
Most employers have disability policies, but many
leaders lack familiarity with proper documentation
requirements and contact information for HR represen-
tatives who can help staff understand their options.

Supervisors should have these conversations with
staff in one-on-one meetings as soon as they're ready to
return to work. The goal is to create an environment
where staff feel comfortable discussing issues and
asking to get needs met, preventing isolation
and absenteeism.

Addressing Workplace Stigma

Staff often fear that bringing up mental health issues
may cause drama or put them at risk of termination—
sadly, even today, they are sometimes right. Outdated
messages like "leave home at home" coerce workers to
suffer in silence. They may know colleagues who were
written up for being late, reprimanded for low production or even fired when struggling through mental
health crises.

Employees might feel unsupported by co-workers—

perhaps they've heard a colleague be mocked for showing vulnerability or overlooked for promotions based on mental health struggles they've worked to conceal. When company culture allows demeaning language like "she's crazy" or "he's psychotic," organizations increase stigma and cause harm.

The fear of stigma—the sum of the negative attitudes and beliefs people hold about mental illness—is real and damaging, economically as well as emotionally. Few of us want to be seen as weak and fragile at work, especially by colleagues and managers who may have little understanding of what's happening. But by focusing on supportive versus punitive measures, organizations boost morale and keep operations running optimally.

After witnessing the mass shooting and returning to work, my life entered a chaotic new phase. A series of life-changing events would follow me for the next few years, making work-life balance a constant struggle. I would need time off, support and flexibility. Knowing Aaron was supportive went far in ensuring I felt comfortable approaching him when major life events occurred.

The foundation my parents had built—their consistent support, their advocacy, their modeling of resilience—meant that I knew what healthy support looked like and could recognize it when Aaron provided it. But not all employees bring this template to work. Some may never have experienced the kind of reliable support I grew up with, making it even more crucial for leaders to demonstrate trustworthiness consistently and explicitly.

The Cost of Poor Judgment During Recovery

PTSD affects parts of your brain responsible for judgment, and I made a perfect example of poor decision-making during recovery. Despite having supportive leadership at DDI, I decided to change jobs while still processing trauma.

My therapist questioned my decision. "Times of stress aren't really great times to take on big changes, like career changes," she said. "Are you sure you want to do this?"

I didn't want to hear it. "I made a promise to myself that since I had the chance to live, I'm going to take every opportunity I can. I really think I need a change."

I thought that if I had a major change in my day-to-day work life, I wouldn't constantly think about the shooting. I thought I could leave the past behind and create new memories. Plus, there was the perk that no one at my new job knew about the shooting—I wouldn't have to feel *damaged* around them.

Upon arriving at Grubhub, I realized I'd made a mistake. The work wasn't right for me. Instead of networking and building relationships, I was isolated, spending time reviewing documents alone. I wasn't meeting new people or attending events. The flashbacks returned with full force.

Looking back, I wonder: if DDI had a more supportive and detailed trauma recovery plan in place, would I have stayed? Could something as simple as monthly check-ins with a designated manager have made a difference and saved both me and DDI the trouble of my leaving? I was a dedicated staff member whose knowledge and experience couldn't be replaced.

For leaders, this illustrates a crucial principle: Employees recovering from trauma may make impulsive decisions that seem irrational. Rather than simply accepting their resignations, consider whether enhanced support might address underlying concerns and retain valuable team members.

Building Resilience Through Community

After the shooting, many people set up Facebook groups for survivors as a way to connect and support each other. Since Route 91 festival attendees traveled from across the country, an in-person support group would have been impractical, but social media provided realistic and meaningful connection opportunities.

In these groups, people expressed various coping strategies. Some were going to therapy or finding healthy outlets like journaling. Others were meditating or using art to express emotions. Some, like me, were able to return to somewhat normal lives and feel safe and supported. Others couldn't leave their homes out of fear.

There was one post that really bothered me: *I don't know about you all, but I can't leave the house. I'm terrified of it happening again. I don't think I'll ever be able to get back to normal.*

This post made me sad and also uneasy, as if I might fall into this depression if I didn't keep moving forward. I was determined not to live in fear. I began finding coping skills I knew had worked for me in the past—running became a crucial outlet. As long as my feet were pounding the ground and my heart rate was elevated from exertion, I was free from thoughts of the shooting.

My ability to identify and use healthy coping strategies came directly from watching my mother navigate challenges throughout my childhood. She had shown me that difficulties could be overcome, that persistence paid off and that asking for help was a sign of strength rather than weakness. Not everyone brings these templates to trauma recovery.

I took courageous steps toward healing my fears. About a year after the festival, Jason Aldean revisited Orange County. While he didn't call this show a reunion, there was a feeling it was meant to be just that. "Let's finish this set!" concertgoers said while making toasts. Some wore custom shirts reading "We are here to finish what we started."

"You are heroes and survivors!" Jason said as he came onstage. The crowd roared. Tears streamed down faces as he started playing. It was surreal hearing his voice. I felt strong and supported. The victims were united and forever bonded over history we'd all like to forget.

However, as I looked around, I saw pain and suffering. People were mourning. While the show united us, it couldn't bring back lives lost. Many people used alcohol to numb feelings of pain. More people than I'd ever seen were in the medical tent receiving treatment for alcohol overuse.

Witnessing their trauma made me realize how far I'd come. I wasn't completely healed—flashbacks still surfaced occasionally. I still had safety concerns and would forever have an exit strategy. But I was slowly moving forward with a baby, a thriving career and determination not to allow fear to control me.

The Strategic Value of Proactive Care

I feel grateful I was able to continue working without too much interference from my PTSD symptoms. I knew I could've gone to my bosses at any time and received needed support. But it shouldn't be solely the employee's responsibility to identify what they need at that moment—they might not know.

Having witnessed so many struggling, I realized people may not be able to express their needs. They might struggle to ask for time off for therapy or self-care. They might not know how to get workplace support. Maybe they couldn't return to work at all.

Prioritizing help for employees going through trauma is essential for successful returns to work. When staff feel cared about, they're motivated to complete projects and resume normalcy. Caring for employees also results in better engagement—when they feel seen and heard, they approach leadership immediately instead of isolating and retreating.

When employees feel supported, it reduces burnout. Other staff members understand that the company supports those in need and step up to help instead of feeling dumped on. Having a caring company improves recruitment and retention—when employees feel valued, they want to work there and continue working there.

This type of care takes effort, thoughtfulness and proactivity, but creates successful returns to work and less disruption for companies. This is essential for productivity and bottom lines.

Over the following years, I would need my bosses to show up and support me—not just because of the shooting, but for pregnancy leave, life changes like buying a house and the loss of my father. These are just things *I* experienced. Imagine the life changes an entire workforce might experience simultaneously: divorce, caregiving responsibilities, sudden illness or financial crisis.

My father, who had never missed a soccer game and always listened to my radio shows, who had taught me that I could count on people to show up when it mattered—his death became another test of whether my workplace could provide the kind of consistent support my family had always given me. The organizations that passed that test earned loyalty that extended far beyond any contractual obligations.

If you're a leader, you can be certain that life changes are happening to your employees and will impact work. Supporting employees during both major and minor life changes doesn't just mean it *feels good* to work with your organization—it means employees will likely stay productive, dedicated and motivated even during unexpected life stress.

Having awareness and plans in place is a vital step to maintaining success for everyone involved. The alternative—watching valuable employees leave during their most challenging moments—is far more costly than the investment in comprehensive support systems.

Remember: Trauma doesn't discriminate based on how strong someone's foundation appears to be. The employee who grew up with incredible support can be

just as profoundly affected as someone whose childhood provided fewer resources. But those early foundations do influence how people interpret and respond to
organizational support during a crisis. When you
provide the kind of consistent, reliable support that
some employees learned to expect in childhood and
others never experienced, you're not just helping them
through   current   difficulties—you're   potentially
building new templates for what safety and trustworthiness look like in professional relationships.

∾

KEY TAKEAWAYS

Prepare before crisis hits: Develop systematic
return-to-work protocols rather than improvising
responses during emotional times when clear thinking
is compromised.

Normalize different recovery patterns: Some
employees will discuss their trauma openly; others will
remain private—both approaches are valid and require
tailored support.

Create clear communication channels: Establish
who employees contact, what documentation is
required and what support is available to eliminate
confusion during crisis.

Address workplace stigma proactively: Counter

"leave home at home" mentalities that force employees to suffer in silence and ultimately leave.

Recognize trauma's cognitive impact: Employees may struggle with focus, decision-making and judgment during recovery—these are biological responses, not performance issues.

Document everything: Clear policies protect both employees and organizations while ensuring consistent support across all situations.

Invest in retention: The cost of replacing experienced employees far exceeds the investment in trauma-informed support systems.

Monitor for secondary departures: One employee's unaddressed trauma can trigger others to leave if they perceive lack of organizational support.

3

LEADING THROUGH THE VALLEY

How did I not die? After the shooting, I grappled with thoughts like *How was it that I was able to walk away from that horrific scene?* The incident at Route 91 was the largest mass shooting by one lone gunman in American history. A thousand rounds of ammunition were shot, hitting people all around me.

I remember looking over my bloodstained body and thinking, *How is this not my blood?* The fact that I survived still shocks me. I thought back to the man next to me who couldn't get up and run because he had been shot. "Run!" I said. But he couldn't. He just lay there.

Before I knew it, my husband grabbed my hand, and we fled.

Why couldn't he run? Should I have stopped to help that woman who fell? Did I do all that I could?

These thoughts consumed me. I came to understand them as a normal part of a terribly complex and unpredictable process every leader must understand: grief in the workplace.

Understanding Grief in the Workplace

You don't have to experience trauma to experience grief. The loss of a loved one, the death of a friend or even the passing of a pet can cause grief. Grief can also stem from loss of things or events—loss of a job, a divorce or even something that *didn't* happen, like being unable to become pregnant after years of trying.

For leaders, understanding grief isn't optional—one way or another, it's inevitable. When examining grief, medical professionals widely adopt a model developed by Elizabeth Kubler-Ross called "the five stages of grief."[7] This model explains that anyone experiencing grief may move through five major emotions: denial, anger, bargaining, depression and acceptance.

The stages of grief have no beginning or end date, and there is no order in which the stages will reliably present themselves from person to person. This unpredictability creates management challenges you must prepare for.

For example, an employee who has just experienced the loss of their longtime spouse might find themselves spending all their time tidying up the house, paying bills, selling things and cleaning out closets. Instead of allowing their feelings of grief to be present, they avoid them with busywork—which can be a tricky form of denial. At work, this might manifest as obsessive perfectionism or taking on excessive responsibilities.

This denial might lead to overwhelming feelings of sadness and depression. When someone's world changes forever, the most mundane activities—like attending meetings or completing reports—can become fraught and painful experiences.

While no one I knew personally died in that shooting, I experienced profound and sometimes overwhelming grief. I grieved for the strangers I didn't know and never will. I felt crushed by the loss of so many innocent people, an impact that will reverberate through families and communities for decades to come.

With that overwhelming loss came a phenomenon called *survivor guilt*—something that can occur in employees who make it through layoffs, workplace accidents or other traumatic and destructive events when their colleagues don't. It can cause similar depressive symptoms to those associated with PTSD, including flashbacks, intrusive thoughts or feelings of worthlessness, anger and irritability.

I personally coped by talking about the incident. I needed to process my feelings and say what was on my mind. My friend Lauren started a group chat with me and a few other friends who were all at the event. We would keep in touch and check in on one another. If a triggering news report or image was released, we checked in on one another.

More than anything else, survivor's guilt comes from a sense of isolation and loneliness. One reliable, time-tested antidote? *Do something good for someone else.* Following the shooting, I saw many of my fellow victims find ways to cope by serving humanity— creating GoFundMe campaigns, making and selling art with proceeds benefiting families, giving back in whatever capacity they knew how.

While I coped with my grief and survivor guilt, I also made a choice to *live.* I didn't die in the shooting. I got that most precious of things: a second chance. Suddenly, living my life to the fullest was no longer simply a goal. Now, it felt like more of a *responsibility*— to myself, my loved ones, my community and my world.

When Personal Grief Meets Professional Responsibility

Little by little, I began to heal my trauma, grief and survivor guilt. But grief wasn't done with me yet. In 2019, two years after the shooting and only six months into my new daughter's life, my dad passed away. He'd been in and out of the hospital with heart issues, but somehow, I never expected him to die until the moment it happened.

The day my dad died, we were set to fly out for a visit to my brother's house. My daughter had a cold, so we decided to stay home and canceled our flights. Later, while eating lunch at Islands—my favorite restaurant from my high school and college years—I got the call.

"This is Dad's nurse," I said to Kevin as I nervously answered the phone.

"Carly," the nurse said frantically, "I just got here. Something is wrong. Can you please come over right away?"

I immediately hung up and called my mom, who was working at least 30 minutes away. We both raced toward my dad's house. Seconds before I entered his driveway, I heard the sirens of an ambulance. I looked up just in time to see it streak by, followed by a sheriff's patrol car at top speed.

When I arrived at the house, my dad's nurse waited outside, deeply upset.

"Do you think my dad will make it to the hospital?" I asked.

The nurse shook his head. I knew at that moment that he was gone.

"I was talking with your dad about surfing," the nurse told me. "He started to laugh and then clutched his heart." My dad had a blood clot that exploded in his heart.

My dad was more than a father—he was my coach, my champion and my biggest fan. Whether it was on the field, in my personal life or navigating my career, he was always there with the advice I needed. He was the person I called whenever I had problems I knew I couldn't solve myself. When I was faced with a new job opportunity, I would ask him what to do.

"Look at the bigger picture, Carly," he would say. "What's best for you and your family?" He would remind me that if a new raise or company perk came with too much life stress, then maybe it wasn't the right move.

I was relieved that he would no longer be sick or have to deal with poor health. But I also felt selfish. I didn't want to let him go. Living without his support was going to be the most difficult thing I faced.

Processing his death was brutally sad, and like most grieving people, I had to do this on the go, while taking care of my baby and going to work, because life doesn't stop for grief. This reality faces every employee you lead.

Leading Through Loss: A Manager's First Test

Having lived through my own traumatic experience, I could no longer ignore the signs of trauma and grief in others. While working at Grubhub, I supervised a dispatcher named Matt who liked to pass wisdom along to younger co-workers. He considered himself a mentor and took this role seriously.

One weekend, one of Matt's mentees, Xavier, was in a fatal car accident. This was a huge loss for our whole team—but especially for Matt. It was also my first loss as a leader, supervising nine employees in Orange County and Southern California. I was nervous but also ready for the challenge.

It was important for me to process the death with respect and support the team, especially Matt. I brought the team together and gave them space to talk about what happened. I acknowledged the difficulty of moving through grief and offered resources for counseling support. I made sure everyone had details of the funeral arrangements and made it clear that if they wanted to go, they could. Our team sent something to Xavier's family to let them know how much he meant to all of us.

I could tell Matt was taking Xavier's loss especially hard. I decided to keep a close eye on Matt to make sure he was coping and to watch for signs of stress or faltering mental health. I met with him one-on-one and allowed him to use our time together to vent his complex range of emotions. I created a safe place for him and let him know he could always come and talk to me.

We didn't replace Xavier's desk or title right away. We left his desk as it was and kept his position vacant for some time. I didn't want the team to feel like Xavier was just a number, someone who could easily be replaced.

Looking back, there were steps I could have taken to honor Xavier while also ensuring the team felt supported. If I were to give advice to someone else handling this situation, I would suggest that they perhaps have quarterly lunch meetings in memory of the employee, place pictures of him around the office or host an annual memorial service.

I did the best I could at the time, and I learned from this experience about the strategic importance of grief leadership.

Building Organizational Grief Competency

It can be hard work to truly support someone dealing with grief—and it's the right thing for employers to do. The *worst* thing management can do for a grieving employee is to pretend everything is fine and normal.

A manager may do this out of fear of bringing up pain or saying the wrong thing. In most cases, people experiencing grief aren't expecting anyone to string together perfect words. They just want to know they are supported.

True leaders must learn to face discomfort head-on. They must show staff they care, first by acknowledging the loss affecting the team and the people involved.

To support another human through devastating loss

is to understand that grief is a difficult, unpredictable process. The key is patience. When employers understand that staff might be grieving for long periods, they can readjust expectations to help meet the needs of employees, employers and customers alike.

There are many ways companies can address grief strategically:

1. Leaders can educate themselves about how grief works and its impact not just on employees who experience it, but on everyone around them. Despite the intensity of profound grief, it is a nearly universal experience—something any employee could go through at any time. As with trauma, it's a *when*, not an *if*.

2. They can review the company's grief and loss policies. Are they strong enough to match the company's culture and mission? Regarding time off, is paid leave offered? How much? What are the stipulations? Are there other policies that apply to grief? Do they reflect the company's promise to support its employees?

3. Bosses must allow themselves to let go of any assumptions they might have around trauma and grief. This frees them to develop empathetic listening skills and determine what the employee really needs.

When it comes to grief, there are no timelines, benchmarks or KPIs. For some people, the loss of a beloved pet may provoke overwhelming grief. As leaders, we must check our assumptions about grief at the door. Saying things like, "Work will be a nice distraction" or "I know exactly what you're going through" may not be helpful at all.

Managers can show support by asking the employee what they need and how they are coping, giving them a sense of agency and belonging. This can even lead to breakthrough ideas for company policy. If a team member requires significant time off, the team can decide how to best redistribute the workload until the employee can return and fully engage.

Grief can result in lack of focus and motivation at work, perhaps especially for people working remotely or in isolated environments. Rather than expecting employees to function at full capacity while coping with grief, leaders must get creative. Work hours can become more flexible. Responsibilities can be shifted or redelegated.

Grief is more than most leaders can handle alone, so it's important to have reputable resources on bereavement and loss. In some cases, employees may want to take advantage of protections offered by the Family and Medical Leave Act (FMLA), which helps employees balance work and family responsibilities through reasonable unpaid leave.[10]

If a company experiences shared, collective loss—death of a co-worker, natural disaster or other grief-triggering event—managers must implement company-wide plans to support staff. This could include hosting grief awareness groups led by qualified mental health professionals, planning memorial services on-site, allowing staff to attend funerals or honoring the event in ways that feel validating to those affected.

Case Study: Proactive Grief Leadership

My friend Brian owns large apartment complexes in several states. He contacted me after a beloved project manager—someone he'd never met in person but who was adored by tenants—had a brain aneurysm on-site and died. Many witnesses, including residents, saw this happen. Everyone in the community was devastated.

"Everyone loved being around her," Brian explained. "I think the community is really upset by this tragedy. I didn't know her at all, but I feel like I should do something. Do you have any suggestions?"

I explained what I did when Xavier died—and what I wish I'd done—to support my team. It would have been easy for Brian to send the family a card and hastily move on. He sensed, though, that caring for his employees and tenants would be more involved.

I advised Brian to open communication lines and offer proactive support. First, gather everyone for a memorial service. Find reputable grief information and provide appropriate resources to staff. Contact witnesses and check on their needs. Make it clear to anyone involved that he's willing to listen and provide support with no expectations or judgment.

Finally, don't rush to fill her position immediately. Find creative ways to get work done without minimizing the loss of someone who can never really be replaced. Create distance from the event rather than carrying on with *business as usual* while so many were grieving.

Because of Brian's proactive approach, everyone involved felt supported. Without this approach, unsupported employees and customers would likely have experienced festering resentment, slowly losing respect for leadership and weakening team unity.

Supporting employees through grief comes down to communication. A leader with strong communication skills who engages in good faith will find it easier to solve any problem. In company cultures that prize strong communication, employees support each other and find innovative solutions to whatever challenges grief may bring.

Collective Trauma: Leading Through Crisis

In 2020, as you may recall, the world shut down. The COVID-19 pandemic was a vector for collective trauma and grief throughout the world, revealing everything we took for granted. Everything in our day-to-day lives was upended.

It was also the year I discovered I was pregnant with my second child. While headed to a St. Patrick's Day party, I suddenly thought, *I'm feeling* way *off*. The heightened sense of smell and emotional sensitivity signaled what I suspected: pregnancy.

What is happening? I thought. There was a global pandemic going on, and I was pregnant. With new COVID protocols, there was extra stress. News outlets constantly reported that hospital beds were impossible to obtain. I didn't want to have my baby in a hospital hallway.

At every doctor's appointment, the nurse took my temperature. I would hold my breath, waiting to hear the *beep*. Kevin couldn't be with me for any appointments. It was just me and my soon-to-be son, isolated from family, hoping there was a safe path for him to arrive.

Working through COVID was complicated—and I thrive in situations that seem difficult to others. After my dad died, I decided to leave Grubhub. Aaron and Adam had called and asked me to return to DDI as director of operations, managing 20 to 30 employees.

DDI was in one of the few industries that could use the pandemic to help others thrive. Our main job was to deliver things—literally helping stores get goods to people by contracting, managing and paying drivers. Businesses like restaurants were now even more dependent on our services.

I immediately got busy troubleshooting logistics problems businesses were facing. Our current model didn't account for much beyond restaurant deliveries. We had to rework business practices for everyone involved—restaurants, drivers and customers.

I partnered with delivery companies to help them ramp up driver fleets quickly. For those who had never delivered goods, they could rely on my team to get set up and integrated quickly. We were no longer just supporting food delivery, but bringing laptops to college students, medications to pharmacy customers and more.

Because so many people had been laid off, we had a new pool of drivers to hire from. Delivering was something they could do safely with minimal infection risk. We contracted with thousands of drivers during this time. I felt good about finding work and financial stability for so many people.

We surveyed our drivers and asked what they liked about delivering. Many reported they felt great when they could deliver lifesaving medications to the elderly or get a laptop to a student in need. They felt like they were part of the solution.

I'm a born problem-solver. Whether providing jobs for unemployed people or helping businesses keep their doors open, the work we did made me feel like I could make a real difference. In a way, I was able to turn my pain into purpose.

One of the biggest challenges was transitioning to off-site work. I wrote blog posts on establishing proper boundaries to work productively from home. I implemented morning check-ins and after-work meetings where staff shared how they were feeling and identified impediments to getting work done at home. I made sure my team felt supported and took time to process all that was happening.

The Business Case for Grief-Informed Leadership

COVID-19 caused collective grief like most of us have never seen or imagined. As employees felt pressured to resume normalcy and return to offices, they brought their grief back to work with them.

The World Economic Forum reports that much of the grief associated with the pandemic remains locked up inside offices, teams and workplaces worldwide.[11] That buildup of grief is leading to burnout, endless fatigue, loss of focus and diminished employee engagement—all negatively impacting productivity.

Employees who report feeling cared for are "60 percent more likely to remain at a company for three or more years." These same employees are "90 percent more likely to describe their companies as an exceptional place to work" to others and suggest they apply.[12]

These supportive measures benefit all of society. By implementing healthy cultures, managers develop stronger and more productive companies that better

serve the world. When employees feel safe and validated in their struggles and grief, they're more eager to
communicate effectively, work collaboratively and
resume their roles at full capacity when they can.

Studies continuously show that when employees
and customers feel supported, they return that loyalty.
Companies exist to make money, and the bottom line
matters—but companies are made of people, and
people aren't machines.

Leadership means helping people become not just
great employees, but happy, healthy humans as well.
The strategic investment in grief-informed leadership
pays dividends in retention, productivity and organizational reputation that far exceed the costs of
support systems.

~

KEY TAKEAWAYS

Grief follows no timeline or hierarchy: A pet's
death may impact an employee as profoundly as losing
a parent—avoid making assumptions about "appropriate" grief responses.

The five stages are not sequential: Employees may
cycle through denial, anger, bargaining, depression and
acceptance in any order, multiple times, creating unpredictable workplace behaviors.

Proactive communication prevents secondary

trauma: Address loss openly rather than pretending normalcy, which can retraumatize grieving employees and damage trust.

Create meaningful memorial practices: Simple gestures like leaving desks vacant temporarily or holding memorial services demonstrate organizational values and support healing.

Flexibility is a strategic investment: Redistributing workload and adjusting expectations during grief prevents permanent talent loss and builds long-term loyalty.

Collective trauma requires systemic response: Events like COVID-19 create organization-wide grief that demands comprehensive support strategies, not ad hoc solutions.

Documentation protects everyone: Clear grief policies, FMLA procedures and resource lists prevent improvised responses during emotional times when clear thinking is compromised.

Supported employees become loyal advocates: Organizations known for caring during a crisis attract and retain top talent while building positive reputations that enhance recruitment and business relationships.

4

BEYOND COMPLIANCE: BUILDING EXCELLENCE IN WORKPLACE PROTECTION

The years following the shooting became a masterclass in understanding the true costs of unpreparedness. As I navigated therapy sessions, flashbacks and the slow work of rebuilding my sense of safety in the world, one question haunted me with increasing urgency: How many of the people who died that night might still be alive if basic safety protocols had been in place?

This isn't the comfortable distance of academic analysis or the luxury of theoretical debate. This is the harsh clarity that comes from running for your life through chaos that could have been prevented, from watching people fall because no one had planned for the moment when everything went wrong. My trauma and grief have become unwelcome teachers, showing me exactly how leaders can—and must—protect their people better.

The revelation that transformed my perspective wasn't complex: Making safety a genuine priority doesn't require enormous resources, disruptive transitions or big sacrifices in other areas. It's a matter of reallocating energy and practices more effectively, of moving from the bare minimum of compliance to the higher standard of actual protection. But first, you have to confront the uncomfortable truth about how most organizations currently approach safety—and why that approach is failing the people who depend on it.

When I look back on the Route 91 festival, what disturbs me most isn't the evil of one man's actions— that was beyond anyone's control or understanding, perhaps even his. What keeps me awake is recognizing how better preparation might have prevented tragic losses that had nothing to do with the shooter's intent and everything to do with systemic failures in crowd management, communication and emergency response. Obviously, hindsight provides information no one had at the time. But when I recall that weekend with the hard-earned wisdom of someone who survived it, the gaps in safety planning become painfully clear.

There were 22000 people packed into that festival venue on the night of October 1. Picture that number— nearly the capacity of Madison Square Garden, spread across an outdoor space with limited exits and barriers designed more for crowd control than emergency evacuation. When the first shots rang out at 10:05 pm, cutting through the music like thunder through silence, most people didn't immediately recognize the sound for what it was.

The sound seemed to come from everywhere and nowhere. In those first crucial seconds, when survival often depends on immediate, correct action, thousands of people stood frozen in confusion. Many thought it was fireworks—a reasonable assumption at an outdoor music festival. Others wondered if something had gone wrong with the sound equipment. The delay in recognition costs precious seconds that, in crisis situations, can mean the difference between life and death.

When Jason Aldean and his band suddenly fled the stage, the crowd's confusion transformed into terror. But even then, the panic was unfocused and thus dangerous. No one knew where the gunfire was coming from, but everyone assumed the threat was at ground level—someone in the crowd with a weapon. This misconception sent people running in every direction, including some who ran directly toward the Mandalay Bay hotel, unknowingly moving closer to the actual source of danger 32 floors above them.

"He's after me!" people screamed as they pushed past others, their voices raw with panic. "Here they come!" The crowd psychology of terror took hold, creating the illusion that shooters were everywhere, pursuing individuals through the crowd. This false perception turned an already deadly situation into a stampede where people became threats to each other in their desperate attempts to escape a danger they couldn't locate or understand.

The physical infrastructure of safety—or lack thereof—became brutally apparent as thousands of people tried to flee simultaneously. The exits that should have been clearly marked and easily accessible were nearly impossible to find in the darkness and chaos. Gates and barriers that had been designed to keep concertgoers contained within the 15-acre venue now trapped them, blocking alternative escape routes that might have dispersed the crowd more safely.

When we did locate functional exits, they revealed the fatal flaw in the venue's emergency planning: They were either blocked, inadequately sized for mass evacuation or led to dead ends that forced people to double back into the danger zone. Imagine trying to pour 22000 people through a handful of narrow openings while gunfire continues overhead—the physics alone should have told planners this system would fail catastrophically under pressure.

But perhaps most disturbing was watching the complete breakdown of human guidance systems during the crisis. Security guards, many of them young and clearly undertrained for anything beyond checking tickets and breaking up minor altercations, stood paralyzed by the magnitude of what was unfolding. I watched one guard pointing vaguely toward an exit as if we were leaving a routine event, his casual gesture surreal against the backdrop of screaming and gunfire.

"Do you not know that there's someone shooting?" I yelled at him as Kevin and I jumped over obstacles and pushed through the stampede. The guard's expression was blank, almost peaceful—perhaps shock had taken over, rendering him unable to process the terror of what was happening around him. In that moment, when clear leadership and decisive action could have saved lives, the people responsible for crowd safety had become obstacles themselves.

The human cost of these failures continues to haunt me. People didn't just die from gunshot wounds that night—they died from being trampled by crowds of people running for their lives with nowhere to go. They died because they couldn't find exits in the dark. They died because no one had prepared for the moment when 22000 people would need to escape simultaneously from a space designed to contain them. Some fell in the middle of the venue and couldn't get back up, becoming perfect targets for a shooter they never saw, in a location that should have been their refuge.

Looking back, I wonder with an intensity that sometimes takes my breath away: *Could some of these casualties have been prevented?* Not the shooting itself—that required a level of evil that no safety protocol addresses.

But the secondary deaths, the trampling victims, the people who died because they couldn't find their way to safety in time? Those losses feel preventable in a way that haunts every conversation I have about workplace safety.

For leaders reading this, understand that this question isn't academic—it's urgent and immediate. Every day you delay implementing comprehensive safety protocols is another day your people remain vulnerable to preventable harm. There are steps every organization can take to be safer, practical measures that don't require enormous budgets or dramatic restructuring. But first, you must recognize the significance of safety as more than a compliance checkbox, and from there, with focused effort and genuine commitment, you can implement protocols that protect lives and prevent the kind of chaos that turns manageable emergencies into tragedies.

This chapter will show you how to build safety systems that actually work—not just on paper, but in the terrifying moments when lives depend on preparation, training and leadership. You'll discover why most current workplace safety measures are inadequate, how to implement protocols that mirror the effectiveness of school and airline safety systems and, most importantly, how to create a culture where safety becomes a competitive advantage rather than a grudging obligation.

Because here's what I learned in those seven

minutes of gunfire: When catastrophe strikes, you find out instantly whether your safety measures were real or just performance. The difference between the two isn't just a matter of liability or compliance—it's a matter of who goes home to their families and who doesn't. And that difference is entirely within your control as a leader.

The question is whether you'll choose to act on that control before the moment when lives depend on it.

Learning from Educational Excellence

My two children are now in school, where safety is taken very seriously. When it comes to children, society doesn't hold back on safety measures. All K-12 schools have rigorous safety standards that reassure parents their children are receiving protective care.

Schools prioritize safety by keeping doors locked at all times, requiring identification when picking up children and having set procedures that enhance safety and well-being. Most importantly, schools have safety drills.

Safety drills enhance student safety by creating familiarity with escape routes, assembly points and communication procedures. These drills increase the chances of quicker and more organized responses in the event of danger. The types typically practiced are fire drills, earthquake drills and active-shooter drills.

The more you rehearse a safety plan, the more

likely it is that the plan will be committed to memory. Through repetition, participants internalize their roles and understand proper responses. This makes actions feel automatic, increasing response time if high-stress situations or emergencies occur.

When teachers and leadership guide children through safety steps until they literally *know the drill*, they prevent the sort of mass chaos that leads to further casualties when disasters take place.

For an example of safety taken seriously, look to commercial aviation. Before any flight is ready for take-off, flight attendants guide passengers through safety steps. Everyone knows the phrase "put your mask on first" because of repetitive instructions given to every single person who gets on a plane.

When practice drills are used properly, they effectively prevent accidents and death. Not only does everyone have a rehearsed plan for safety, but drills help work out kinks. They ensure equipment works properly, help determine blocks to exit and expose flaws in even the best-laid plans. This creates opportunities to enhance safety *before* crisis occurs.

For corporate leaders, the lesson is clear: If kindergartners can master comprehensive safety protocols, your workforce can too.

The Corporate Safety Gap

Neither DDI nor Grubhub practiced safety drills. In fact, none of the jobs I've had have ever gone over fire escape routes, earthquake drills or what to do in the event of an active shooter. Most businesses have safety requirements they must follow—like posting building maps or having clear exit signs. This is the bare minimum.

There may have been maps posted in offices where I worked, but I can't recall a single time that anyone brought them to my attention or took them seriously. In my experience, regularly practiced drills are just not part of corporate practice.

Later in my career, when Walmart acquired DDI, I was required to watch a safety training video. This training was prompted by numerous violent attacks on Walmart premises. According to *Business Insider*, Walmart—the largest retailer in the United States—saw the most gun violence, including 310 firearm-related incidents and 89 deaths.[13]

The video had an acronym meant to be used as a strategy to maintain safety during active-shooter situations. It showed a reenactment of a disgruntled man with a gun entering the workplace. Actors portraying employees hid from him or used desk supplies to defend themselves—throwing staplers, phones or purses while trying to run to safety.

I found the video deeply disturbing. No one mentioned there was an active-shooter portrayal or said anything specific about the content. Instead of teaching me what to do, it just portrayed a scary scene of something that could happen at work. I didn't want to hear those sounds, see those images or spend any time in that world.

Like many other employees, I put the video on in the background and let it play through while I answered emails and completed other tasks. When it was over, I hit "submit" to receive my "safety credit," barely remembering the acronym or what it stood for.

For leaders, this represents a critical failure. Safety training that traumatizes employees while failing to educate them serves no purpose except checking compliance boxes. Effective safety programs require thoughtful implementation that actually prepares people for crisis while protecting their mental health.

Building Comprehensive Safety Programs

Practicing safety is such an easy and essential part of managing workplace crisis that kindergartners do it regularly. There are many ways leaders can incorporate effective safety practices at work.

My first recommendation is to assign this task to someone who will take it seriously and incorporate it into company culture. This could be a manager, someone in human resources or an employee with the right combination of skills, knowledge and enthusiasm. The person identified can take on the role of chief safety officer.

This person needs a comprehensive understanding of the company's safety priorities, which must extend far beyond posting emergency exit signs and hoping for the best. The role demands three critical areas of expertise that can mean the difference between coordinated response and deadly chaos.

Professional Safety Qualifications and Training

Your chief safety officer must receive formal safety qualifications and training from security professionals—not just online modules or compliance videos, but hands-on instruction from experts who understand how people actually behave during crises. This isn't about checking boxes; it's about building expertise that saves lives when seconds matter.

To illustrate how these principles play out in practice, let me share some composite scenarios drawn from the experiences of safety professionals across various industries. While the specific details have been altered to protect organizational privacy, these examples reflect real patterns of failure and success that safety experts encounter repeatedly. They demonstrate why the difference between adequate and excellent safety planning isn't academic—it's measured in lives saved or lost when preparation meets crisis.

Consider what happened at one corporate headquarters when a disgruntled former employee attempted to force entry during business hours. The designated safety coordinator had completed all required training modules but had never practiced applying that knowledge under pressure. When the threat materialized, she froze, unable to remember whether the protocol called for lockdown or evacuation. Employees received conflicting instructions over the building's communication system, with some floors locking down while others evacuated, creating confusion that could have proved fatal if the situation had escalated.

Professional training goes beyond memorizing procedures—it builds the kind of muscle memory and decision-making capability that functions even when adrenaline floods the system. Security professionals teach safety officers how to rapidly assess threats, coordinate with law enforcement, manage crowd psychology during evacuations and make split-second decisions when standard protocols don't fit the situation.

This training must be refreshed regularly because emergency response skills atrophy without practice. The safety coordinator who completed certification three years ago but hasn't participated in realistic scenario training since then is operating with outdated skills and potentially dangerous overconfidence. Professional trainers use simulation exercises that replicate the chaos, noise and time pressure of actual emergencies, preparing safety officers for the disorientation they'll experience when crisis strikes.

Building Layout and Emergency Route Mastery

Understanding your building's layout and design to determine the safest exit routes during crisis requires more than glancing at floor plans—it demands intimate knowledge of how the physical space will behave when filled with panicked people trying to escape at once.

At one financial services firm, the safety officer had identified primary and secondary exit routes according to building codes, marking them clearly on emergency maps posted throughout the offices. But during a bomb threat evacuation, she discovered that her carefully planned routes created dangerous bottlenecks. The main stairwell, adequate for normal traffic, became a crushing hazard when 400 employees tried to use it simultaneously. Meanwhile, a service corridor she'd dismissed as too narrow actually provided faster egress for small groups, but employees didn't know it existed because it wasn't part of the official evacuation plan.

Effective safety officers conduct physical walk-through assessments at different times of day and under various conditions. They understand how locked doors after hours change evacuation options, how construction projects might block previously viable routes and how seasonal factors like snow-covered fire escapes affect emergency planning. They know which stairwells have the widest landings for disabled employees who might need assistance, which exits lead to genuine safety versus parking garages that could become traps and how to coordinate with building management to ensure emergency systems function properly.

This knowledge extends to understanding sight lines and communication challenges within the space. A safety officer who hasn't considered how cubicle walls might prevent employees from seeing exit signs, or how the building's acoustics might distort emergency announcements, is planning for perfect conditions that don't exist during actual crises.

Most critically, they must understand crowd flow dynamics—how people move in groups under stress, where fatal bottlenecks typically occur and how to design evacuation procedures that account for human psychology rather than just regulatory requirements. The exit route that works perfectly on paper might prove deadly when filled with frightened people who can't think clearly enough to follow posted directions.

Individual Employee Needs Assessment

Determining employee needs, including understanding disabilities and mobility limitations, requires systematic assessment that goes far beyond compliance with Americans with Disabilities Act requirements. This is about ensuring that every person in your organization has a viable path to safety during emergencies, regardless of their physical capabilities or personal circumstances.

Imagine the leaders of a technology company learning this lesson during a fire evacuation. They discovered that three employees—one using crutches due to a recent surgery, another with severe anxiety about enclosed spaces and a third who was deaf and hadn't received visual emergency notifications—were left behind because the evacuation plan hadn't accounted for their specific needs. The employee with crutches couldn't navigate the crowded stairwell at the pace required for safe evacuation. The anxious employee had locked himself in a bathroom rather than enter the packed stairwell that triggered his claustrophobia. The deaf employee never received notification that evacuation was necessary because all emergency communications were audio-only.

Effective safety officers maintain confidential databases of employee needs that might affect emergency response, updated regularly as circumstances change.

This includes temporary conditions like injuries, ongoing medical treatments that might affect mobility or cognitive function during stress and personal factors that could influence emergency behavior. They work with employees to develop individualized evacuation plans that account for specific limitations while maintaining dignity and privacy.

This assessment process must address psychological as well as physical needs. Employees with PTSD from previous traumatic experiences might react differently to emergency alarms or evacuation procedures. Those with anxiety disorders might need specific reassurance or alternative evacuation routes that avoid crowded areas. Recent immigrants might not be familiar with American emergency procedures, while employees with language barriers might need emergency communications in multiple languages to respond appropriately.

The safety officer must also understand how personal relationships affect emergency behavior. Parents will prioritize getting to their children, often abandoning workplace evacuation procedures to drive to schools. Employees with elderly parents or disabled family members might refuse to evacuate if they're worried about loved ones. Recognizing these human factors allows safety officers to plan for the reality of how people actually behave during crises rather than how policies assume they should behave.

This holistic, comprehensive understanding enables safety officers to design inclusive emergency procedures that account for the full spectrum of human needs and responses. When crisis strikes, this preparation ensures that protective measures actually protect everyone— not just the young, healthy employees who can run down stairs quickly and think clearly under pressure.

From there, the chief safety officer can begin developing a comprehensive disaster-preparedness plan that serves as the foundation for all organizational safety initiatives. This isn't a document that should gather dust in filing cabinets—it's a living framework that guides decision-making, resource allocation and response protocols when crisis strikes.

The Occupational Safety and Health Administration (OSHA) has developed "Recommended Practices for Safety and Health Programs" that provide an evidence-based foundation for organizational safety planning.[14] Rather than creating guidelines from scratch, smart organizations leverage this research-backed framework that has been tested across thousands of workplaces and refined through decades of real-world application.

OSHA's approach recognizes that effective safety programs serve multiple strategic purposes simultaneously. Their primary goal is preventing workplace injuries, illnesses and deaths—the devastating events that can destroy lives in an instant and create ripple effects that extend far beyond the immediate victims. But the framework also acknowledges the broader impact of safety failures, addressing the profound suffering and financial hardship these events cause for workers, their families and employers.

This comprehensive perspective matters because it helps leaders understand that safety isn't just about compliance or liability protection—it's about protecting the human foundation upon which all organizational success depends. When employees suffer preventable injuries or deaths, the costs extend far beyond insurance claims and legal settlements. Organizations lose institutional knowledge, team cohesion and the trust that enables people to focus on innovation and growth rather than basic survival.

OSHA's recommended practices provide chief safety officers with systematic approaches to hazard identification, risk assessment, employee engagement and continuous improvement that transform safety from reactive damage control into proactive organizational strength. The framework emphasizes that the most effective safety programs are those that engage employees at all levels, recognize that frontline workers often have the best insights about operational risks and create cultures where people feel empowered to speak up about potential hazards before they become actual emergencies.

For organizations developing their disaster-preparedness plans, OSHA's framework serves as both foundation and road map—providing proven principles while allowing for customization based on specific industry risks, organizational culture and operational realities.

These recommended practices use a proactive approach to managing workplace safety and health. They include prioritizing the role of safety managers, engaging employees in participation, identifying workplace hazards and methods for preventing hazards. OSHA also emphasizes the importance of education and ongoing training to keep these standards fresh for employees.

When taking a proactive approach, management can prevent more damage from occurring. Had a proactive approach to safety been used on the night of the shooting, I know that lives could've been saved.

Implementing Effective Safety Drills

Drills are an important part of staff safety, and different scenarios require different responses. Severe weather drills help employees know what steps to take during earthquakes, tornadoes or other extreme weather events. This might include moving away from windows, bookcases and large objects or identifying safe locations—under desks, tables or along interior walls.

Lockdown drills or intruder drills prepare

employees for scenarios involving active shooters or intruders. First, staff can learn preventative measures, like common warning signs to look for. Is there a disgruntled customer? Is a co-worker in a violent relationship? Is there a sudden change in a colleague's behavior or mood?

Management should let staff know that if they see or even *feel* that something is "off," they *must* reach out to proper people as soon as possible, whether a supervisor, HR or law enforcement.

Next, employees should be trained on:

- Proper exit procedures
- Escape routes
- Potential hiding places

Staff can learn how to secure their work areas and find the nearest safe space to hide. Basic measures, like ensuring staff members keep their employee badges with them at all times and keeping all doors locked throughout the day, can delay and even prevent intruders from entering the workspace.

If companies want to take things further, these drills can include education on self-defense. Self-defense boosts confidence, enhances decision-making skills and promotes a sense of security while at work.[15] Self-defense skills not only show employees how to keep themselves safe during violent attacks but also help employees feel empowered and in control.

Fire drills should be comprehensive plans that address every aspect of emergency response, not the perfunctory exercises most employees endure, where people casually stroll to the nearest exit and mill around parking lots without purpose. Effective fire safety requires systematic planning across four critical areas, each of which can determine whether an emergency becomes a manageable evacuation or a deadly catastrophe.

Communication: Clear Command Structure

Who will be in charge of communicating that there is a fire? This isn't just about pulling alarm handles—it's about establishing clear command authority and communication protocols that function even when normal systems fail. The wrong approach treats communication as automatic, assuming building alarms and PA systems will handle everything. The right approach recognizes that emergency communication is active leadership requiring human judgment and redundant systems.

Imagine an accounting firm. A small electrical fire starts in a supply closet on the third floor during lunch hour when most employees are away from their desks.

The first person to notice smoke pulls the fire alarm, but the building's automated system only provides a generic evacuation tone—no information about the fire's location, severity or specific evacuation routes. Employees on the first floor hear the alarm but continue working, assuming it's another false alarm triggered by someone burning lunch in the break room microwave. Meanwhile, employees on the fourth floor begin evacuating through the main stairwell, unaware they are heading toward the floor where smoke is beginning to spread.

The communication breakdown continues as the designated safety coordinator tries to provide updates over the PA system. Her voice is barely audible over the alarm noise. Employees can't understand whether they should shelter in place, evacuate immediately or avoid certain areas of the building. The fire department arrives to find some people still at their desks while others cluster in the main lobby, unsure of whether it's safe to exit the building.

Contrast this with a law firm that has implemented comprehensive communication protocols. When a fire starts in its electrical room, the safety coordinator immediately takes control of building communications, overriding the generic alarm with specific instructions: "This is not a drill. We have a confirmed fire on the second floor. All employees below the second floor should exit immediately through the north and south exits. Employees above the second floor should use the west stairwell only and avoid the main stairwell."

Each floor has designated communication wardens with two-way radios who confirm receipt of instructions and report on evacuation progress. When the west stairwell grows crowded, floor wardens coordinate to stagger evacuation timing, preventing dangerous bottlenecks. The safety coordinator maintains constant communication with arriving firefighters, providing real-time updates on which areas have been cleared and where employees might still be located.

Evacuation: Practiced Procedures Under Pressure

What steps do staff need to take to exit the building safely? This goes far beyond knowing where the exits are—it requires understanding how to move efficiently as a group, how to assist others who need help and how to adapt when primary routes become unavailable. Poor evacuation planning treats employees as individuals responsible for getting themselves out. Effective evacuation planning recognizes that people become part of a collective system that must function cohesively under extreme stress.

Imagine a marketing agency that discovers its evacuation weaknesses during what should be a simple, routine drill. Employees know the locations of emergency exits, but no one has practiced moving through them as a group. When 200 people try to use the main stairwell simultaneously, the evacuation slows to a halt as people stop to chat with colleagues, check phones or grab personal belongings from desks. The stairwell becomes so congested that employees on upper floors are effectively trapped behind slower-moving groups, turning a five-minute evacuation into a 20-minute ordeal that would likely prove fatal in an actual fire.

The agency's "solution" is to post signs reminding people to move quickly, but this misses the fundamental problem: They have never practiced evacuation as a coordinated group activity. During their next drill, people still cluster in doorways, hold doors for friends coming from other departments and treat the exercise as a social opportunity rather than emergency training.

For a more effective response, take the composite example of a construction company that treats evacuation drills as precision exercises requiring coordination and timing. The leaders assign specific roles to employees on each floor: door monitors who ensure areas are clear before leaving, crowd managers who prevent bottlenecks at stairwell entrances and sweep teams who conduct final checks of bathrooms, conference rooms and break areas where people might be trapped or hiding.

During drills, employees practice moving in organized groups rather than as individuals. Floor wardens count heads and report numbers to the safety coordinator, enabling real-time tracking of evacuation progress. When congestion develops in stairwells, trained employees redirect traffic to alternative routes. The company regularly times its drills and works to improve evacuation speed while maintaining safety, treating emergency response as a skill requiring constant refinement.

Safety: Strategic Assembly Areas

Determining safe zones so employees know where to gather once they've exited requires understanding how emergency scenes actually function and what hazards exist outside the building. Many organizations designate assembly areas based on convenience rather than safety, creating new dangers during the moments when people are most vulnerable, as the following composite examples will demonstrate.

Now, imagine an office building that designates its main parking lot as the emergency assembly area because it's the largest open space near the building. During a fire drill, employees dutifully gather there as trained, but the safety coordinator realizes too late that the parking lot is directly adjacent to the building's main electrical transformers and natural gas connections. If an actual fire spread to these utilities, the "safe" assembly area would become the most dangerous location on the property. Additionally, the parking lot is accessed by the same road used by emergency vehicles, creating potential conflicts between evacuating employees and arriving firefighters.

The building's emergency planning also failed to consider weather factors. During a winter drill, employees stomp their feet in the parking lot for 15 minutes in freezing sleet, with no shelter or provisions for extended waiting. Several people with health conditions become ill from exposure, requiring medical attention that further complicates the emergency response exercise.

By contrast, imagine a pharmaceutical company that designs its assembly areas strategically, considering multiple factors beyond simple proximity. Safety leaders designate primary assembly areas at least 150 feet from the building, upwind from potential chemical hazards and accessible without crossing emergency vehicle routes. Secondary assembly areas are identified for use during severe weather, including arrangements with nearby businesses to provide temporary shelter if needed.

This company's assembly areas include supply caches with basic emergency provisions: battery-powered megaphones for communication, first aid supplies, blankets for weather protection and bottled water for extended evacuations. Floor wardens carry clipboards with employee rosters, trained to conduct accountability checks immediately upon reaching assembly areas, identifying missing persons quickly enough for rescue teams to respond effectively.

First Aid: Medical Response Readiness

There are two important items to consider when it comes to medical response readiness and first aid:

- Does someone need CPR training?
- Does the building have basic first aid items available and easily accessible?

Emergency medical needs don't pause during evacuations—in fact, the stress of emergency situations often triggers medical crises that require immediate response. Organizations that treat first aid as an afterthought discover too late that emergency services may be delayed or overwhelmed when most needed.

A consulting firm learned this lesson during a fire evacuation when an employee with a heart condition collapsed in the stairwell, blocking the exit route for dozens of people behind him. No one present had medical training beyond basic first aid, and the building's first aid supplies were locked in a cabinet on the first floor—inaccessible to people trapped in the stairwell. Employees spent precious minutes trying to decide whether to move the unconscious man, potentially worsening his condition, or wait for paramedics who couldn't reach him through the crowded evacuation route.

The firm's emergency planning had ignored the reality that medical emergencies often occur during evacuations when stress, physical exertion and anxiety peak simultaneously. This left the company with no protocols for handling medical crises during evacuations, no trained responders positioned strategically throughout the building and no medical supplies accessible from evacuation routes.

One manufacturing company took a comprehensive approach to emergency medical preparedness, training 20 percent of its workforce in CPR and basic first aid, with trained responders distributed across all shifts and building locations. Automated defibrillators and trauma kits were placed at strategic locations, including stairwells, exits and assembly areas—places where medical emergencies commonly occur during evacuations.

Its evacuation procedures included specific protocols for medical emergencies: Trained responders carried radio beacons so they could be located quickly by emergency services, evacuation routes had designated bypass procedures to maintain flow around medical incidents and assembly area managers were equipped to provide triage and coordinate with arriving paramedics.

Accommodating Individual Needs: Universal Emergency Design

All safety plans and drills need to make accommodations for employees who have physical disabilities or other concerns that would prevent them from following standard procedures. The question "How will someone get downstairs if they are in a wheelchair?" represents just one aspect of designing emergency systems that work for everyone, not just the young and physically capable.

Consider a software company that discovered the limitations of its accommodation planning when its team attempted to evacuate an employee who used a wheelchair from the fourth floor during a drill. The plan called for two volunteers to carry the wheelchair down the stairs, but they had never practiced this procedure. The volunteers were quickly exhausted by the weight, the wheelchair user felt unsafe and undignified, and the evacuation route became blocked for other employees. The drill revealed that their "accommodation" was actually dangerous for everyone involved.

The company had made the common mistake of treating accessibility as an add-on to standard procedures rather than designing inclusive systems from the beginning. Its emergency planning assumed that disability accommodation meant asking nondisabled people to provide assistance, without considering whether those helpers would be available, willing or capable during actual emergencies.

On the other hand, one financial services firm designed universal emergency procedures that enabled everyone to evacuate safely and independently. It installed evacuation chairs at strategic stairwell locations, trained multiple employees in their use and practiced regularly to build competence and confidence. For employees with hearing impairments, the company installed visual alarm systems and assigned visual notification responsibilities to floor wardens. Employees with anxiety or cognitive processing differences received advance notification of drill schedules and alternative evacuation routes that avoided crowded areas.

Most importantly, the leaders recognized that disability accommodations benefit everyone during emergencies. The clear visual signals helped all employees in noisy environments, evacuation chairs could assist anyone who became injured during evacuation and alternative routes provided options when primary exits became blocked. By designing for universal accessibility, they created more robust emergency systems that improved safety for their entire workforce.

Trauma-Informed Safety Training

When implementing safety plans, staff should use trauma-informed language and approaches as much as is realistically possible. This means approaching staff to discuss plans and drills *before* practicing or implementing them. As I mentioned before, it's likely that someone in the office has experienced trauma. Trauma can lead to PTSD, which can cause symptoms of flashbacks, panic attacks and feelings of terror.

If possible, a person experiencing PTSD needs to know if a trigger is coming (the sound of something that mimics gunfire, discussions about violence, being enclosed in small areas or not being able to access exits, for just a few examples).

It's leadership's job to discuss possible triggers to ensure that employees are aware they might occur and have the option to opt out, take less intense training or have time to recover after practicing.

For instance, it would have been helpful for me to know that the video I was being asked to watch at Walmart depicted an active-shooter incident. I could have avoided that part or been excused from watching altogether.

Implementing safety standards isn't a one-and-done thing. Companies that prioritize safety must make sure safety becomes a normal part of organizational culture. Leaders can do this by having staff-wide safety training regularly to review plans, practice and implement changes as necessary.

Consider hiring outside consultants to assess plans and ensure there aren't blind spots. Professionals can lead practice drills or offer self-defense classes that include managers too—building trust and collaboration.

There's no shortage of companies that specialize in helping large or small organizations with safety. A quick search lists an array of safety specialty services: self-defense teachers, safety coordinators, security solutions and many more. There's an entire industry of security specialists ready to consult with companies to help increase and maintain employee safety.

There are even companies that help businesses incorporate mass texting services. These can be very effective in communicating with staff during workplace crises. Mass notification systems enable leaders to connect, inform and respond within seconds during emergencies. Different codes for different emergencies can be determined, making it clear to employees what the emergency entails and exactly which plan of action follows.

The Business Case for Workplace Safety

Statistics suggest many Americans feel unsafe at work, creating serious business implications that extend far beyond simple survey numbers.[16] These figures represent millions of employees who arrive at work each morning carrying invisible weights of fear, hypervigilance and anxiety that affect every aspect of their professional performance.

The Erosion of Psychological Safety Through Language

Seventy-eight percent of workers witness disrespectful or insensitive language at work, leading to feelings of threat. Picture the administrative assistant who flinches every time her manager raises his voice during meetings, not because he's addressing her, but because his tone reminds her of childhood experiences with an explosive father. Consider the marketing coordinator who stops contributing ideas after hearing colleagues dismissed with language like "That's the dumbest thing I've ever heard" or "Are you kidding me with this?"

This isn't about political correctness or oversensitivity—it's about the biological reality of how threatening language affects the nervous system. When employees regularly witness verbal aggression, even when it's not directed at them, their brains begin categorizing the workplace as potentially dangerous. They start scanning for signs of impending conflict, diverting mental energy from creative problem-solving to threat assessment. The results show up as decreased innovation, reluctance to take risks and the kind of corporate culture where people stay quiet instead of speaking up about problems that could sink companies.

The cumulative effect builds like sediment in a riverbed. One harsh comment might be forgiven, but months of witnessing dismissive language, public humiliation and verbal hostility create environments where employees operate in constant low-level fight-or-flight mode. They begin making career decisions based not on growth opportunities, but on psychological survival.

When Home Violence Follows Employees to Work

Seventy-five percent of domestic violence victims experienced harassment from their abuser at work. This statistic represents people like the retail manager whose ex-husband calls the store dozens of times per shift, demanding to speak with her and becoming increasingly aggressive when employees refuse to put him through. It includes the accountant whose abusive partner shows up at her office building, waiting in the parking garage or lobby, turning her workplace into an extension of the terror she faces at home.

For these employees, work could represent sanctuary—a place where they can focus on professional tasks and build financial independence that might eventually enable them to escape dangerous relationships. Instead, their abusers systematically destroy even this refuge, ensuring that trauma follows them everywhere they go. The harassment might involve constant phone calls that disrupt meetings, surprise visits that force embarrassing explanations to colleagues or cyberstalking through work email and social media accounts.

The ripple effects extend throughout the organization. Colleagues witness the distress but often don't know how to help, creating awkward tension and whispered conversations. Productivity suffers as the targeted employee struggles to concentrate while monitoring for signs of the abuser's presence. Security becomes complicated when the person posing a threat has detailed knowledge of the employee's schedule, workplace layout and daily routines.

These situations require sophisticated organizational responses that balance employee safety with practical business operations, yet most companies have no protocols for addressing domestic violence spillover into workplace settings.

Growing Fears Among Frontline Workers

Fifty-eight percent of frontline employees believe that the threat of physical harm is growing. These are the retail workers who serve customers face-to-face, the healthcare employees who work with patients in crisis, the service industry staff who deal with increasingly volatile public interactions. They experience firsthand the escalating aggression that has become common-place in customer service environments.

Imagine a grocery store cashier who tenses every time a customer approaches, unconsciously assessing whether this interaction might turn violent over mask policies, coupon disputes or simple misunderstandings. Feel the anxiety of the hospital receptionist who has learned to position herself near panic buttons because patients' family members have become increasingly threatening when they're frustrated with wait times or treatment decisions.

These employees go home each night carrying the stress of hypervigilance, never knowing which routine interaction might explode into dangerous confronta-tion. They develop coping mechanisms like choosing workstations near exits, keeping personal phones easily accessible and mentally rehearsing escape routes. This constant state of alertness is exhausting, leading to burnout rates that devastate industries already strug-gling with staffing shortages.

The growing threat isn't imaginary—it's docu-mented in rising rates of workplace violence, increas-ingly aggressive customer behavior and the normalization of hostility in public interactions. Front-line employees feel abandoned by organizational lead-ership that expects them to absorb this abuse as part of their job responsibilities.

The Exodus of Young Talent

Nearly a third of Gen Z employees have turned down or switched jobs because of safety concerns. This generation, having grown up with school lockdown drills and mass shooting alerts, brings different expectations about workplace safety than previous generations. They're not willing to accept environments where personal security is an afterthought.

These young professionals ask questions during interviews that older generations never considered: What are your active-shooter protocols? How do you handle workplace harassment? What security measures protect employees working late or in isolated areas? When organizations can't provide satisfactory answers, talented candidates accept offers elsewhere.

This represents a fundamental shift in employment negotiations. Previous generations might have prioritized salary, benefits or advancement opportunities above safety considerations. Gen Z candidates treat physical and psychological safety as nonnegotiable baseline requirements, the foundation upon which other job factors are evaluated.

Their departure from unsafe workplaces isn't dramatic—it's quiet and systematic. They don't stage protests or file complaints; they simply update their résumés and find employers who take security seriously. Organizations that ignore these safety expectations wake up to discover their youngest, most technologically adept employees have migrated to competitors who better understand modern workplace safety requirements.

The Mass Departure of Unprotected Workers

Over 50 percent of workers who feel their employers do not prioritize their safety plan to leave within a year. This statistic represents the largest voluntary exodus of talent in recent business history—employees abandoning organizations not because of money or career advancement, but because they don't trust their employers to protect them.

These departures follow predictable patterns. First comes the growing awareness that the company treats safety as a legal compliance issue rather than a genuine priority. Employees notice the outdated emergency procedures, the broken security systems, the dismissive responses to safety concerns. They observe management's reluctance to invest in protective measures or training.

Then comes the active job search, conducted with a level of urgency typically reserved for escape rather than career advancement. These employees aren't looking for better positions—they're looking for safer ones. They research potential employers' safety records, ask detailed questions about security protocols and prioritize workplace protection over salary increases.

Finally comes the resignation, often delivered with polite explanations about "new opportunities" that mask the real reason: loss of faith in the organization's commitment to employee welfare. These departures drain institutional knowledge, disrupt team dynamics and send clear messages to remaining employees about what they should expect from leadership.

The replacement costs extend far beyond recruitment and training expenses. Organizations lose the trust of remaining employees, who interpret each safety-motivated departure as confirmation of their own vulnerability. The cycle accelerates as more people conclude that their employers prioritize profits over protection, leading to the kind of workforce instability that can cripple competitive advantage.

∼

WHEN COMPANIES DON'T TAKE security seriously, it can inflict serious consequences: higher turnover, lower morale and barriers to recruitment. Employees want to work in places where they know they can be safe.

My friend Lee works in the security solution industry, developing top-notch security solutions for businesses and corporations. He spends time researching events in which things went wrong, then develops solutions to prevent them from happening again.

One day he told me about a bank shooting where an intruder walked in during daytime hours and held employees at gunpoint. "A lot of the employees were able to run out of the building and get to safety," he explained. "But they didn't have a plan once they exited. They just ran to the nearest safe place, like their car or another building across the street."

"While all the employees inside the bank knew what was going on, others not working on that floor were clueless about what was happening. An employee of the bank who was outside at the time walked right into the front door where the active shooter was standing with his gun. She was shot several times."

This story illustrates how lack of comprehensive safety planning can lead to preventable casualties. If the employee had been trained in what to look out for, could she have been saved? Could mass-text services, clearly marked safety zones or training on situational awareness have prevented this tragedy?

The story also demonstrates how lack of safety standards can do *emotional* damage. While working at Walmart, I was aware of store shootings. A store manager friend shared that his team was expected to clean up the mess after an event, including blood and other gruesome details that staff were not prepared for or trained in. When retelling this, he became emotional. It was clear this task left many people feeling traumatized. Some quit on the spot. Others tried to return to work but found they were too scared or triggered.

In traumatic scenarios like these, leadership has a responsibility to support staff. I don't believe security standards were purposefully omitted from company policy. It wasn't a lack of *care* but a lack of *understanding*. The people in charge just didn't have the tools or proper procedures in place.

While we may not be able to prevent disasters, we can create more robust plans. Security drills, safety plans and solutions save lives. Furthermore, they increase the likelihood that employees can return to normal, healthy lives.

Reimagining HR as Safety Champions

A well-educated human resources department can play a vital role in organizational safety. Every staff member will have different feelings about safety, depending on their individual life circumstances and temperaments. For me, safety is a top value. For others, it might be an afterthought.

A company can cultivate positive relationships between HR and staff by establishing open-door policies. Staff can be educated that HR isn't only there for punitive measures but as a resource for all questions and concerns at work. HR can work together with staff to create anonymous reporting systems so employees can report concerns without fear of retaliation.

When managers have so many important tasks to complete each workday, safety might seem like one more item at the bottom of the never-ending list. It might even seem wasteful to spend time on safety— especially when doing so doesn't produce direct revenue increases.

But, as someone who's lived through the largest mass shooting in American history, I can assure you that the importance of safety is vital. It can be lifesaving. By taking these measures, leaders create work climates that are not only safe but caring and helpful.

Employees want to work for leaders who care about their safety and prioritize their health and well-being. And if a crisis *does* occur on company time, everyone will be glad they practiced drills and knew what to do.

Building a Culture of Shared Responsibility

We are *all* responsible for cultivating a culture of safety in our communities, at work and in our personal lives. When we take safety seriously, we start to see how simple it is to get smart and stay safe.

We owe it to survivors to look out for each other, pay attention when given safety instructions and be mindful enough to notice when something is off. We can encourage leaders to enforce safety standards, letting them know we're interested and open to learning about ways to keep ourselves safe at work and beyond. For leaders, this means moving beyond viewing safety as a compliance requirement to embracing it as a competitive advantage. Organizations known for prioritizing employee safety attract top talent, reduce insurance costs, avoid costly litigation and build reputations as employers of choice.

The investment in comprehensive safety programs —from designated safety officers to regular drills to trauma-informed training—pays dividends in employee retention, productivity and organizational resilience. When employees feel protected, they perform better. When they feel valued, they stay longer. When they feel prepared, they respond more effectively during actual crises.

Being safe costs very little to implement, but the failure to prioritize safety can cost everything. As leaders, we have the opportunity to transform our organizations into places where people don't just work—they thrive knowing they're protected by leaders who truly care about their welfare.

◈

KEY TAKEAWAYS

Designate a chief safety officer: Assign safety

responsibility to someone with expertise, authority and genuine commitment to organizational protection rather than treating it as an afterthought.

Move beyond compliance to excellence: Basic requirements like exit signs aren't enough—implement comprehensive drill programs that mirror educational best practices and actually prepare people for crisis.

Use trauma-informed training approaches: Warn employees about triggering content and provide alternatives for trauma survivors during safety training to avoid retraumatizing vulnerable staff.

Invest in professional consultation: External security experts can identify blind spots and provide specialized training that internal staff cannot, ensuring comprehensive protection.

Implement mass communication systems: Real-time notification capabilities can prevent confusion and secondary casualties during crises by providing clear, immediate guidance.

Create psychological safety around reporting: Anonymous systems and open-door policies encourage employees to report concerns without fear of retaliation, enabling proactive threat prevention.

Practice makes permanent: Regular drills commit safety procedures to muscle memory, enabling automatic responses during high-stress situations when clear thinking is compromised.

Address both physical and emotional safety:

Consider the mental health impact of safety protocols and provide support for employees processing traumatic scenarios to maintain psychological well-being.

Market safety as competitive advantage: Publicize your safety commitment to attract talent and reassure stakeholders that you prioritize human welfare over mere profit margins.

5

HOW ORGANIZATIONS CAN CULTIVATE POST-TRAUMATIC GROWTH

The fluorescent lights hummed overhead as I stared at my computer screen, the cursor blinking in the empty email I'd been trying to write for 20 minutes. Three weeks had passed since the Route 91 shooting, and I was back at work, supposedly functional, supposedly healing. But the truth was messier than my professional facade suggested. Every unexpected sound—a door slamming, someone dropping a stapler, the coffee machine gurgling to life—sent electricity through my nervous system, pulling me back to that night when gunfire shattered everything I thought I knew about safety.

I was drowning in plain sight, surrounded by colleagues who wanted to help but didn't know how, managing a workload that felt impossible when my brain kept replaying seven minutes of terror on an endless loop. The person who had walked into this office before October 1—confident, focused, eager to please—felt like a stranger I'd once known but could no longer access.

That afternoon, while I sat hunched over my desk feeling particularly defeated by my inability to concentrate on a simple project timeline, my co-worker Adam approached with the careful expression people wear when they're not sure if you're going to break down in front of them.

"How are you feeling?" he asked, settling into the chair beside my desk. "I know it can't be easy."

His kindness almost undid me. I looked up from the screen where I'd been pretending to work and felt the familiar tightness in my throat that preceded tears I couldn't afford to shed during business hours.

"Not so good," I admitted, my voice barely above a whisper. "I can't stop thinking about the shooting, and I've lost a lot of focus here. I feel like I'm letting everyone down."

Adam leaned forward slightly, his expression thoughtful rather than pitying. "Carly, listen to me. This is just a season of hardship. Things will change soon, like they always do. You won't feel like this forever."

Seasons. The word hit me with unexpected force, not because it was particularly profound, but because it reframed everything I'd been experiencing through a lens I hadn't considered. I sat there for a moment, letting the metaphor settle into the chaos of my thoughts.

Growing up in Southern California, I'd never experienced the dramatic seasonal changes known to other areas of the continent—no snow-covered winters giving way to explosive springs, no autumn leaves marking time's passage with vivid transitions. Our seasons were subtle: slightly cooler temperatures, different flowers blooming, rain patterns shifting almost imperceptibly. But I understood the concept intellectually, and more importantly, I understood it emotionally from life's rhythm.

There had been difficult seasons before this one. The season when I was diagnosed with dyslexia in elementary school and struggled to keep up with reading assignments while my classmates seemed to effortlessly absorb information that felt like code to me. The season when I was laid off from a job I'd loved, spending months questioning my worth while watching my savings dwindle. The season when my father's business struggled and our family faced financial uncertainty that cast shadows over dinner conversations and Christmas mornings.

Each of those periods had felt permanent while I was living through them. The dyslexia diagnosis had seemed like a life sentence of academic struggle. The job loss had felt like professional failure that might define my career forever. My father's business troubles had created a family atmosphere of tension that seemed like it might never lift.

But they had all passed. Not quickly, not easily, not without leaving marks on who I became—but they passed. Spring had followed winter, even when I couldn't imagine warmth returning to the frozen ground of my circumstances.

Adam's simple observation—that this was a season, temporary by definition—offered something I desperately needed: a framework for survival that didn't require me to fix everything immediately or pretend the trauma hadn't happened. It acknowledged the reality of winter while promising the inevitability of spring.

For leaders reading this, understand that Adam's intervention represents more than compassionate support—it demonstrates a critical business insight. How your organization responds to employees during their darkest seasons determines not just whether they survive the crisis, but whether they emerge from it as exponentially more valuable contributors to your mission. Adam didn't just help me through a difficult period; he accidentally triggered a transformation that would make me a completely different kind of employee—one worth far more to my organization than the person who had walked into that building before the shooting.

You might look at my professional life and divide it into two distinct eras: before October 1 and after. Before the shooting, I was a competent but unremarkable employee. I did what was asked of me, rarely pushed back on decisions I disagreed with and operated from a place of chronic people-pleasing that prioritized harmony over truth. I had ambitions but no real sense of purpose, career goals but no driving passion to achieve them. I was the kind of employee who shows up, does adequate work and blends into the background of organizational life.

I knew I wanted more from my career, but I had no clear vision of what "more" looked like or how to get there. I was caught in that professional limbo that affects millions of workers—dissatisfied with the status quo but too risk-averse to pursue significant change. I avoided difficult conversations, deferred to authority figures even when I suspected they were wrong and measured success by how few waves I made rather than how much value I created.

This version of me was safe for organizations—predictable, manageable, unlikely to cause disruption. But she was also limited, operating far below her potential because trauma hadn't yet stripped away the protective layers of politeness and risk aversion that kept her small.

After the shooting, everything changed—not immediately, not neatly, but fundamentally. Surviving something that killed 60 people and wounded hundreds

more does something to your risk assessment mechanisms.

Suddenly, the professional fears that had once felt
so important—being disliked, making mistakes, facing
rejection—seemed absurdly trivial compared to the
reality of mortality I'd witnessed firsthand.

I had two choices in this new landscape: I could be
led by fear, allowing a stranger's evil actions to dictate
the boundaries of my remaining life, or I could use the
terrible gift of perspective that trauma provides to
become the person I'd always been too scared to be.

The transformation wasn't instant or easy. For
months, I fluctuated between these two possibilities—
some days retreating into hypervigilance and avoidance, other days feeling reckless with newfound
courage. But gradually, with the support of leaders who
recognized what was happening and chose to invest in
my growth rather than simply managing my symptoms,
I began to access capabilities I'd never
known I possessed.

My bosses at DDI didn't just tolerate my healing
process—they actively encouraged me to stretch
beyond what I'd previously thought possible. When
they promoted me from director of operations to vice
president of partnerships, they weren't just giving me a
title; they were betting on the version of me that trauma
was uncovering. This new role required skills that the

pre-shooting me would have found terrifying: forming relationships with other industry leaders, gaining their trust, advocating for company positions in high-stakes negotiations, speaking with authority on subjects where I was still learning.

These capabilities didn't come naturally—believing in myself was work I had to do consciously, daily, sometimes hourly. But I had something the old me had lacked: the knowledge that I could survive things that felt impossible. If I could run for my life through chaos and emerge intact, if I could process the kind of trauma that breaks some people permanently, then I could certainly learn to advocate for myself in business meetings.

More importantly, I had leaders behind me who understood what they were witnessing. Aaron and others at DDI recognized that trauma survivors often undergo profound personality changes that can make them exponentially more valuable to organizations— not despite their experiences, but because of them. They saw past the initial period of struggle to the potential that the crisis was revealing in the light.

Knowing my company cared for me during the worst season of my life created loyalty that went far beyond normal employee engagement. When an organization supports you through genuine darkness, when they invest in your growth rather than writing you off as damaged goods, you don't just work for them—you become invested in their success in ways that can't be bought with salary increases or benefit packages.

Looking at life through the lens of seasons transformed my entire outlook on both personal and professional challenges. It became a framework for understanding that difficulty, no matter how intense, carries within it the promise of change. Winter serves a purpose in nature's cycle—it clears dead growth, forces adaptation, prepares the ground for new life. The same principle applies to human experience, and smart leaders understand how to help employees navigate seasonal transitions in ways that unlock unprecedented growth.

Through this seasonal perspective, I moved from post-traumatic stress into something psychologists call *post-traumatic growth* (or PTG)—a phenomenon where people don't just recover from trauma but actually become stronger, more capable and more purposeful than they were before the crisis occurred. This isn't toxic positivity or pretending that pain doesn't matter. It's about recognizing that human beings have extraordinary capacity for transformation and that organizations can either support this process or waste it.

What makes this particularly relevant for business leaders is that post-traumatic growth often produces exactly the kind of employees every organization desperately needs: people who are resilient under pressure, clear about their values, willing to take calculated risks, able to handle difficult conversations and driven by purpose rather than just paychecks. These employees become force multipliers within teams, culture builders who attract other high-performers and leaders who can guide organizations through their own difficult seasons.

The seasonal metaphor that Adam offered me that day became more than a coping mechanism—it became a business philosophy. Just as nature uses winter to prepare for spring's explosion of growth, organizations can use difficult periods to identify, develop and retain their most valuable human assets. The employees who thrive during organizational winters, who grow stronger rather than bitter during difficult seasons, are the ones who will drive success during the abundant seasons that follow.

But this transformation doesn't happen automatically. It requires leaders who understand the difference between managing trauma symptoms and cultivating post-traumatic growth, who can recognize the signs that an employee is ready for significant development and who are willing to invest in people during their most vulnerable moments rather than writing them off as problems to be managed.

In the pages that follow, you'll discover how to identify employees who are primed for post-traumatic growth, how to create organizational cultures that support this development and how to leverage the extraordinary capabilities that often emerge from personal crisis. You'll learn why trauma survivors often become your most valuable team members, how to design career development programs that align with the search for meaning that frequently follows traumatic experiences and how to transform individual pain into organizational purpose.

Because here's what I learned during that difficult season and in the years of growth that followed: The same experiences that break some people forge others into exactly the kind of leaders, innovators and culture builders that organizations need to thrive in an uncertain world. The question isn't whether your employees will face difficult seasons—they will. The question is whether your organization will be the kind of place where winter becomes the foundation for extraordinary spring growth or where potential gets buried under the weight of misunderstanding and missed opportunities.

The seasons themselves will come—trauma, crisis and difficulty are as inevitable as winter. But how does your organization prepare for those seasons, support people through them and help them emerge stronger on the other side? *That* choice is within your control.

Understanding Post-Traumatic Growth as a Business Asset

Following a traumatic event or a series of them, a person can experience, in addition to PTSD, a less-studied phenomenon known as post-traumatic growth. *Psychology Today* defines post-traumatic growth as "the positive psychological change that some individuals experience after a life crisis or traumatic event."[17] It goes on to say that "post-traumatic growth doesn't deny deep distress, but rather posits that adversity can unintentionally yield changes in understanding oneself, others and the world."

PTG survivors recognize and embrace new opportunities. They forge stronger relationships with loved ones and within their communities. They cultivate inner strength through knowledge they have overcome tremendous hardship. Overall, they gain a deeper appreciation for life.

For organizations, this translates into employees who become more resilient, purpose-driven and strategically valuable. I had lived through the biggest mass shooting in US history. Nothing in my work life could be more challenging than what I'd already been through.

I started to change my outlook on work entirely. At DDI, when Aaron told me I'd be running a full presentation at our yearly trade show, I was terrified to speak in front of people. The night before, I couldn't eat, felt nauseous, and my nerves were running wild.

"Please don't force me to do this!" I pleaded with Aaron.

"Carly, you've got this—you know how to present about driver onboarding better than anyone in that room," he said. "Why are you doubting yourself?"

Now, I look back on that feeling and laugh. Gone is the person who was unsure about things and needed constant reassurance. I've developed inner strength. I know I can overcome challenges.

"I miss the nice Carly," a board member said in a meeting recently.

I'm sure you do, I thought. He was talking about me before the shooting—when I would silence my own voice to avoid friction or confrontation. When I neglected to stand up for myself and others. When I didn't advocate for what I knew was right or needed.

When I didn't feel confident enough to speak up, it made things *easy* for my co-workers and board members. They weren't faced with confrontation or pushback and could make whatever decisions they felt best.

Today, I can't imagine not speaking my mind or sharing what I believe is important. I speak up with new boldness. Because of this, my colleagues respect me. My opinion and ideas matter. When I speak up, I have something important to say. I have worked hard to step into my power and gain the recognition I deserve.

After the shooting, I realized that I could handle hard conversations, difficult emotions and conflict. I was no longer afraid to ask for what I wanted. I experienced so much loss, and I knew firsthand just how fragile life can be. I had no choice but to go after what was best for me and my family—and prove I was the best person for the job.

For leaders, this transformation represents exactly the kind of employee you want to identify, nurture and retain. Trauma survivors who experience post-traumatic growth often become your most valuable team members—not despite their experiences, but because of them.

Strategic Employee Development Through Crisis

Helping employees grow is a leader's responsibility with measurable business returns. There are many ways to foster development, but trauma presents unique opportunities.

Since becoming a leader, I've spotted employees who are loyal and dependable and helped them grow. When I was responsible for hiring at DDI, there were important people I wanted on my team. I worked with

Ernesto at Islands, my favorite restaurant from my childhood and a place that honed my work ethic and sense of team camaraderie like few others. He was so easy to work with—willing to listen to my ideas and try new ways of doing things that would ultimately help him improve as an employee. He was loyal, eager to learn and exactly the kind of employee I wanted to work with at DDI.

When I got the chance, I interviewed him and hired him on the spot. He is still working with me today.

When I was hired at Grubhub, there was an employee, Martin, who seemed distant. He was disappointed I was hired because he thought he was next in line for my job. He felt hurt and struggled to stay motivated. He had incredible skills in analytics and data collection, and because of his skills, I knew he was valuable. I worked with him in one-on-one meetings, asking Martin to trust me and reassuring him that I had better plans for him.

He continued to show up and do his job, going above and beyond at times. He helped me with things I couldn't have done myself, like creating systems and spreadsheets that helped us be more efficient. When he was laid off due to a mass budget cut, I was the one responsible for telling him.

"Martin, I know this doesn't seem fair, but you've got to trust me," I explained. "I've already got another job lined up for you at DDI."

I asked Aaron at DDI to interview Martin and gave him a glowing review. DDI hired him—in part because I'd earned their trust through my commitment and resilience.

When I met Sean, he was going through a hard time. He'd just moved to the area to take care of an elderly parent who needed his help. He had been running his own businesses and managing partnerships in the food industry in LA. Despite that, he needed a job close to his parents and was willing to go above and beyond.

"He's perfect for the position. I just have a feeling about him," I explained to Aaron. "He left his successful life behind to come here and care for his parents. That's loyalty! I know he'll be loyal and committed to us too."

"He's a flight risk, Carly," Aaron worried. "What will he do when things resolve and he's no longer needed here?"

"You've got to trust me, Aaron," I pleaded. "I know he's the right person."

Aaron finally agreed and we hired Sean as director of operations—filling my position so I could move into vice president of partnerships.

As a leader, I felt it was important to help employees grow by seeing strengths in them that they might not have seen in themselves yet. With all three employees I hired, they performed beyond expectations. Ernesto is now a senior vice president of operations for a contracting company. Martin is a senior manager working in the e-commerce umbrella at Walmart. Sean works with me at Openforce as a director of client management.

Leaders win when they look to grow the right employees—especially those who've demonstrated resilience through personal challenges.

Identifying Growth-Ready Employees

Leaders can look for specific signs that an employee is ready to move into growth. Some signs include:

- An employee asking for more responsibility
- An employee who exceeds all expectations
- An employee who meets timelines, performs at a high level and makes the job look easy
- An employee who co-workers go to for help or assistance
- An employee who is already leading in some way

A leader will know someone is ready to grow when they are consistently thinking above their paygrade. This employee brings ideas to leadership that maybe haven't been considered. They think about their role in broader terms.

If an employee has a desire to move upward in the

company, the leader can lay out a plan. This could mean assigning projects that demonstrate growth, allowing opportunities to lead and offering encouragement. If there is no option to move upward, the leader can clarify and collaborate on other opportunities for employee satisfaction and fulfillment.

Leaders can offer professional development through extended training and support—outside an employee's regular tasks. If staff have an interest in how another department works, managers can set up training or situations for them to learn. Cross-department training provides better understanding of the inner workings of the company and develops knowledge.

Some organizations improve growth by offering tuition reimbursement or training certifications. This is a valuable benefit that will not only attract the best talent but also develop experts, which improves company growth.

If the company is small, with little opportunity for growth within the organization, leaders can help staff grow in other ways. They can use their network and colleagues to provide additional learning opportunities—like attending seminars and leadership conferences.

When employees have the opportunity for growth, they feel fulfilled. Fulfillment leads to a sense of purpose and meaning. A sense of purpose could matter more than any other perk the company might offer.

A *Forbes* article says that company perks like cars or trips won't matter to an employee if they don't feel passionate and aligned with the work they do.[18] It says that by "having regular conversations, offering job rotations, aligning company values with personal values, fostering curiosity and encouraging continuous learning, employees can find their purpose and stay engaged."

Leveraging Purpose as a Retention Strategy

After the shooting, I began running again. I wasn't just running for exercise, though. I ran because others no longer could. I found that through running, I was able to honor the victims who lost their lives.

Running became not only my greatest coping skill, but one of my driving passions. It was something that helped ease my stress and cope with PTSD, and it added value to my life. In addition to my career, running became a key facet of my post-traumatic growth.

For leaders, understanding that trauma survivors often seek deeper meaning in their work presents strategic opportunities. These employees aren't just looking for paychecks—they're looking for purpose. Organizations that can provide meaningful work and growth opportunities will capture fierce loyalty from employees who've experienced trauma.

There are countless ways to find purpose outside of work, and smart leaders encourage these pursuits. People can find new hobbies or revisit things they used to love, like playing music or painting. Hobbies aren't just for leisure—they are essential acts for personal growth, improving mental health and providing a sense of fulfillment.

When I finished a run, I felt accomplished. It felt good to have control over something when there was so much uncertainty shaping my life. After each run, I felt hope for myself. I would think, *I'm here. I didn't die.*

Leaders and co-workers aren't typically tasked with helping employees find purpose outside of work, but they can certainly help. If you have a colleague who has experienced trauma or loss, you can invite them into your community. Extend an invitation to an art class or cooking seminar. Put together an office bowling league or other sporting event that creates connection and provides the opportunity to learn new skills or find new hobbies.

A leader who influences staff to find meaning and purpose will lead a happy and motivated organization.

The Strategic Value of Mentorship

Continuing to grow my career after the shooting provided my life with purpose and meaning. After someone experiences trauma, finding purpose is such an important aspect of healing—and smart leaders can facilitate this process.

For me, growing my career gave me a sense of control over my fate. I had objectives and goals. These were things I could strive for and accomplish. In addition, the more I moved up the ladder, the more opportunities there were for me to help others. By becoming a manager, I was able to lead people and help them gain knowledge and skills.

I started noticing the people I worked with who believed in me—my cheerleaders—always there helping me grow and advance. Aaron and Adam would encourage me to go for a big pitch or close a deal even when I felt it was out of reach. They taught me that failure was part of learning and that I could learn lessons along the way, no matter what the outcome.

For years, I worked with a man named Jim, an entrepreneur and customer of DDI. He was a major player in our business and someone who could teach me things I had yet to learn. Jim was part of an industry association called ECA: A Delivery Industry Alliance.

Every year ECA hosts a huge conference that invites industry leaders to speak on topics that will promote growth for those working in the field. I loved attending the ECA conference, always knowing I would make great connections and learn new advances in the business.

One year at the conference, I was hanging out with

Jim, and we started talking about the work he does on the board.

"Would you ever consider joining?" he asked. "I think you'd be a great fit, Carly. It's not easy to get in, but I think it's worth trying."

At the time, getting a board position was nearly impossible. The people on the board were influencers and change-makers. Everyone in the industry knew them and hoped to get their assistance and attention. To be among them as a peer would be an enormous vote of confidence for the work I'd been doing.

First, I would need a nomination. Someone with a reputable organization would need to verify that I was worth considering. Next, I would have to be voted in by the association members. The problem was that I would be the newbie running against incumbents.

Adam was willing to nominate me for the position. He wrote me a letter of recommendation, and the next year I went into the running against an incumbent. I lost. I was disappointed, but Jim, along with other board members, encouraged me to continue trying.

"These things take time," Jim explained. "The older board members have been around for a long time, and change is hard. Just don't give up."

I remained committed, and the following year, when it was time to vote again, I submitted my letter of intent for a board position and ran in the election. Once again, I lost. I began to lose hope that being a board member was going to happen for me.

I really wanted this opportunity. After the shooting, my focus was growth. I wanted to grow in my career in all possible ways. I had a renewed sense of vitality. I lived when so many others did not, and I wanted to make my life count.

"Don't give up," Jim offered after I lost again. "An opportunity will present itself."

I had a hard time believing him, but this is why it's good to have a mentor. They can give you hope or believe in you when you cannot see it for yourself.

It wasn't long after my second loss that Jim called.

"Hey, Carly," he said. "One of our board members needs to step down. We need someone to fill in as an interim member until it's time to vote again. Would you be up for the position? There's no election. You'll just step in."

"Yes!" I said with excitement. I knew this was an opportunity to show my strengths.

I stepped in, and just like I'd done since high school, I proved myself through consistently applying my strong work ethic. Right away, I took over the technology committee. The website needed a refresh—but without any disruption for customers. I spent long hours getting things up and running without any issues for ECA or its members.

When it came time for another election, I put my

name in the running—and I was elected! I have been on the board for five years as the technology chair. Today, when I attend ECA conferences, *I* am an influencer in the industry. People look at me with admiration, hoping that I will provide them with a nugget of wisdom.

For leaders, this illustrates the power of strategic mentorship. Jim saw potential in me that I couldn't see in myself. He provided guidance, encouragement and ultimately opportunity. Smart organizations pair trauma survivors with experienced mentors who can help channel their newfound sense of purpose into career advancement.

Implementing Positive Organizational Mindsets

For me, having a positive mindset doesn't mean I don't acknowledge pain and suffering—quite the contrary. Instead, it's a realization that I can't control what happens around me. What I *can* control is how I respond to negative events in my life, the way I perceive hardships and how I handle my emotions when faced with challenges.

According to the Mayo Clinic, there are tested ways to flip your overall outlook from negative to positive on an ongoing basis.[19] As with learning any new skill, it takes practice, understanding and education. One effective approach to shifting your mindset from negative to positive is to first pinpoint a specific area where you seek improvement.

When you spot negative thinking or self-talk in action, you can use *reframing* to try to turn those thoughts from negative to positive. Cognitive reframing is a technique used to shift your mindset so you're able to look at a situation, person or relationship from a different and more useful perspective.

For me, after the shooting, I reframed my thoughts from *these awful feelings will last forever* to *I will get through this*. Instead of thinking, *This meeting is going to be the worst*, try reframing it as *I'm curious to see how this meeting goes*. Just by changing that one simple thought, you send signals to the body to stay calm, reducing stress and providing much-needed comfort.

Solidifying a positive mindset includes daily self-check-ins. Before things spiral—circling around the same worry or fear, compounding anxiety and stress— you can check in with yourself. If your thoughts are stubbornly negative, try a change of scenery. Go for a walk or take a break by engaging a co-worker in conversation.

When I was spiraling at work, I would often get up and walk around the office, reminding myself I was safe and that everything, in that moment, was fine. Or I'd go for a run and process what I was feeling before I reacted.

Finally, and perhaps most importantly, being

around positive people can help improve your mindset. When my mood was low and I was struggling, I had supportive people in my life who would lift me up. My bosses, my co-workers and especially my family helped me maintain a positive outlook. They said things like "You've got this!" when I was questioning myself.

Having a positive outlook or experiencing post-traumatic growth doesn't minimize pain. It doesn't negate its severity or replace hurt with toxic positivity. For me, having a positive outlook was crucial for survival. It was how I managed to take one step at a time in the right direction.

I worked hard to remind myself that I had another chance at life when so many others didn't. I asked myself, *What could I do with this second chance? How will I live out my purpose and turn my pain into something meaningful?*

For leaders, fostering this mindset in your organization creates environments where trauma survivors can thrive rather than just survive. When you teach cognitive reframing techniques, encourage positive self-talk and model resilient thinking, you're not just supporting individual employees—you're building organizational culture that attracts and retains high-performing, purpose-driven talent.

From Individual Pain to Organizational Purpose

When all other resources are exhausted, turning pain into purpose can sometimes be the *only* way people are able to cope. There's no shortage of nonprofits and companies founded by people who experienced trauma. Homeless shelters, recovery houses, veterans' services, animal shelters and gun-control initiatives often develop as a result of the pain of a victim whose life was irrevocably altered by a tragic event.

For the founders of these companies, post-traumatic growth means providing their communities with tools of prevention, education and awareness. Many raise money for charitable donations, help survivors heal from trauma for free and even have voices in politics, all in the interest of making our lives safer.

For organizations, this represents an opportunity to channel employee experiences into meaningful corporate initiatives. When companies create volunteer programs, charitable partnerships or community outreach efforts that align with employee experiences, they tap into extraordinary motivation and purpose.

Smart leaders recognize that employees who've experienced trauma often become passionate advocates for causes related to their experiences. Rather than viewing this as a distraction from work, forward-thinking organizations leverage this passion to build stronger community relationships, enhance corporate social responsibility and create authentic purpose that attracts top talent.

The noise in our minds can swell with doubts, distractions and outside opinions. But here's the truth: Growth happens when you stay focused on your path and keep going, even when no one's watching. It's easy to question if it's all worth it. But if you believe in what you're doing, and you stay committed to the journey, the outcome can be more powerful than you'd imagined possible.

For leaders, supporting employees through this journey—from trauma to growth to purpose—isn't just compassionate leadership. It's strategic business practice that transforms individual pain into organizational strength, creating workplaces where people don't just recover from trauma—they use it as fuel for extraordinary achievement.

~

KEY TAKEAWAYS

Post-traumatic growth is a measurable business outcome: Employees who experience PTG often become more resilient, purpose-driven and strategically valuable to organizations than they were before their trauma.

Identify growth-ready employees through crisis: Look for those asking for more responsibility, exceeding expectations and thinking above their current role—especially those who've demonstrated resilience through personal challenges.

Create purpose-driven development programs: Align career advancement with employees' search for meaning following traumatic experiences to capture fierce loyalty and exceptional performance.

Support both professional and personal growth: Encourage hobbies, community involvement and creative outlets that help employees process trauma while building well-rounded, fulfilled team members.

Implement cognitive reframing in organizational culture: Teach positive mindset techniques that help teams view challenges as seasons rather than permanent states, building organizational resilience.

Foster strategic mentorship relationships: Pair trauma survivors with supportive leaders who can guide them through growth opportunities and help them see potential they can't recognize themselves.

Recognize the "seasons" mindset: Help employees understand that difficult periods are temporary phases rather than permanent conditions, enabling them to maintain hope and forward momentum.

Leverage trauma survivors as organizational assets: Those who've experienced PTG often become exceptional leaders, mentors and culture builders who add extraordinary value to teams.

Channel individual experiences into corporate

purpose: Create volunteer programs, charitable partnerships and community outreach efforts that align with employee experiences to tap into authentic motivation.

Transform pain into competitive advantage: Organizations that effectively support trauma survivors through growth create workplaces that attract and retain purpose-driven, high-performing talent while building authentic corporate social responsibility.

6

VULNERABILITY AND STRATEGIC LEADERSHIP

The fluorescent lights in the office bathroom felt harsh against my reflection as I stared at myself in the mirror, practicing words I wasn't sure I was ready to say. It was my first day back at work after the Route 91 shooting, and I was about to face the inevitable question that every returning employee dreads: "How was your time off?"

How do you answer that question when your "time off" was spent processing the fact that you'd run for your life through a field of bodies while bullets rained down from a hotel window? How do you explain that you'd used your vacation days not for relaxation, but for therapy sessions and sleepless nights replaying seven minutes of terror? How do you bridge the gap between the professional persona your colleagues expect and the fundamentally changed person trauma has created?

Standing there in that bathroom, I was caught between two equally terrifying possibilities. I could pretend nothing had happened, performing normalcy while carrying the weight of unspeakable experience alone. Or I could tell the truth and risk having that truth define every professional interaction for the rest of my career.

The fear of returning to work and telling everyone what happened felt almost as overwhelming as the shooting itself. I wasn't sure how to talk about the tragedy yet—the words felt too big, too raw, too likely to spill out in ways that would make everyone uncomfortable.

I could imagine the awkward silences, the careful way people might start treating me, the whispered conversations that would follow me down hallways. I didn't want people to feel sorry for me or start handling me like fragile glass that might shatter if they spoke too loudly or shared normal workplace stress. The thought of becoming the office tragedy case, the person everyone tiptoed around with careful smiles and lowered voices, made my chest tighten with a different kind of panic.

Even more terrifying was how sharing my story might influence how others perceived me in my role as both an employee and a leader. I had worked relentlessly hard to build professional credibility, to be seen as competent and reliable. What if my trauma overshadowed my capabilities? What if colleagues started questioning my judgment, wondering if someone who'd been through something so extreme could still make rational business decisions?

Like most people, I didn't want to be seen as a *victim* —that label felt like it would reduce everything I was to a single terrible night, erasing years of professional growth and achievement. The word itself seemed to carry implications of helplessness and fragility that contradicted everything I knew about myself. I was a survivor, someone who had faced the unthinkable and emerged intact, but would anyone else see it that way?

The fear extended to my supervisors as well. Would they start assigning me fewer tasks out of misguided concern that I couldn't handle pressure anymore? Would challenging projects be quietly redirected to colleagues deemed more "stable"? The possibility of being professionally sidelined because of something that had actually made me stronger felt like a secondary victimization I couldn't bear.

At the same time, it felt important—necessary, even —not to conceal this part of my life. Hiding such a significant experience felt like living a lie, carrying on conversations about weekend plans and work deadlines while a massive piece of my reality remained locked away. The truth is, experiencing a mass shooting has profoundly altered me. It wasn't something I could compartmentalize or leave at home like a bad mood or personal problem. It was an integral part of my life narrative that had changed how I viewed risk, safety, priorities and the preciousness of ordinary moments.

Every time someone complained about minor inconveniences—traffic delays, meeting room temperatures, coffee machine malfunctions—I found myself recalibrating what actually constituted a problem worth worrying about. When colleagues stressed about project deadlines or presentation anxieties, part of me wanted to share the perspective that surviving actual life-and-death situations provides: Most workplace crises aren't really crises at all.

But how do you share that kind of perspective without sounding dismissive or traumatized? How do you offer the hard-won wisdom that comes from facing mortality without making everyone around you uncomfortable with the weight of what you've learned?

The internal conflict was exhausting. I practiced different versions of the story—clinical and detached, emotional and raw, brief and matter-of-fact. None of them felt right. They either revealed too much or concealed too much, created distance or demanded intimacy, positioned me as a victim or survivor or something in between that had no clear name.

For leaders reading this, understand that this tension between authenticity and professional image represents one of the most fundamental challenges of modern workplace dynamics. In an era where we're encouraged to "bring our whole selves to work," what happens when part of yourself includes experiences that fundamentally challenge assumptions about safety, normalcy and what constitutes appropriate professional conversation?

How do you share meaningful parts of your experience without compromising your authority? How do you model authenticity without crossing boundaries that make others uncomfortable? How do you use personal struggles to build stronger teams without becoming the leader who overshares or makes every situation about their own experience?

The answer, I discovered over years of navigating these waters, lies in understanding vulnerability as a strategic leadership competency, not a weakness to overcome or a burden to manage. But this realization didn't come immediately or easily. It emerged through trial and error, through moments of connection and instances of oversharing, through feedback from colleagues and the gradual recognition that my experience, properly shared, could serve purposes beyond just processing my own trauma.

The first time it came up organically was months later, during a team dinner at Walmart. We were at a restaurant for an off-site meeting, the kind of forced bonding experience that usually involves awkward small talk and carefully neutral observations about food and weather. But something about the casual atmosphere, the wine loosening inhibitions and the genuine curiosity of my new colleagues created a space where deeper sharing felt possible.

We were getting to know one another, moving beyond work roles into the personal stories that make us human. Someone talked about their kids' sports schedules, another shared frustrations about elderly parents and a third mentioned a recent divorce that had upended their living situation. The conversation had found that sweet spot where professional boundaries relaxed enough to allow real connection without crossing into inappropriate territory.

When the attention turned to me, I felt the familiar internal debate: deflect with something safe and surface-level or risk the vulnerability of truth. At that moment, surrounded by colleagues who had shared their own struggles, it felt more honest than frightening to say, "I was in Vegas during the mass shooting."

The reaction was immediate and intense—not the pity or discomfort I'd feared, but genuine concern mixed with curiosity and something that looked like respect. People leaned forward instead of pulling away. The questions came carefully but genuinely: Was I okay? What was it like? How did I get through it?

After I share my story now, people usually want to know more. I've learned to gauge the room, to read faces and body language for signs of genuine interest versus polite obligation. I've always been deliberately sparse with the details, not wanting to bore anyone with a story I've told many times or to traumatize listeners with imagery they didn't sign up for.

But I've also learned to recognize when people want to ask questions without knowing how to do so appropriately—when they're curious but worried about offending me or forcing me to relive painful memories. In those moments, I try to expand the details strategically, sharing pieces that help people feel connected to the experience without overwhelming them with its full horror.

I might mention what a big Jason Aldean fan I am, how excited I'd been to see him perform, how the music had been the soundtrack to what should have been a perfect weekend. Or I'll explain why I ran toward the Tropicana instead of toward other exits, the split-second decision-making that survival requires, the way crisis strips away everything except the most basic human instincts.

This measured approach to sharing creates connection without overwhelming colleagues or compromising professional boundaries. It allows me to be authentic about a formative experience while maintaining the leadership presence my role requires. Most importantly, it models for others that traumatic experiences don't have to be either completely hidden or completely exposed—there's a middle ground where vulnerability serves both personal healing and professional purpose.

But learning to navigate this middle ground took time, mistakes and a fundamental shift in how I understood the relationship between personal experience and professional effectiveness. The journey from fear-based hiding to strategic vulnerability became one of the most important leadership lessons of my career, with implications that extended far beyond my own story to how I support employees, build team culture and create organizational environments where authenticity and excellence can coexist.

In the pages that follow, you'll discover how vulnerability, properly understood and appropriately applied, becomes a powerful tool for building trust, inspiring teams and creating competitive advantages in markets where authentic leadership differentiates successful organizations from those that merely survive. You'll learn to distinguish between strategic vulnerability and problematic oversharing, to recognize when personal stories serve broader purposes and to create workplace cultures where people feel safe bringing their full selves to work without sacrificing professional standards or organizational effectiveness.

Because here's what I learned in that bathroom mirror and in countless conversations since: The choice isn't between invulnerable leadership and unprofessional oversharing. The choice is between authenticity that serves your mission and performance that exhausts your soul. And in a world where employees increasingly demand genuine connection with leaders they can trust, the organizations that master strategic vulnerability will attract and retain the talent that drives sustainable success.

When Vulnerability Meets Professional Opportunity

In 2024, I went to a conference with ECA. I and another board member, Samantha, were there representing ECA in hopes of attracting more carriers and shippers to our platform. Our booth was next to other vendors, and we all talked and mingled throughout the conference.

Samantha noticed that we were next to the same person she had met last year. His name was Lee, and he was the vice president of remote security solutions.

"Carly, this is Lee," she introduced us, and I reached out for a handshake.

"Hello, nice to meet you," Lee said. "I'm getting ready to do a presentation on our security solutions over on the exhibit floor. You should come and watch."

As we got closer, I noticed that he was standing there next to a large TV. I suddenly heard, "Get down! Get down! There's an intruder in the building!"

I immediately froze. A chill ran through my spine. I started trembling.

I turned to Samantha. "Is this happening right now?" I asked in fear.

"Oh, Carly, I'm sorry," she said. "No! This is part of Lee's presentation."

Lee's company helps organizations prepare for active shooters by providing security systems and resources. He was demonstrating prevention methods —state-of-the-art technology like gun detection software, security monitors and alarm systems that connected directly with 911 in case of emergency.

Hearing the words *get down* had triggered me so much that I couldn't watch the rest of Lee's presentation. I walked away and went back to my booth, reminding myself that I was okay and that everyone was safe.

A little later, Lee approached our booth again. "Was my presentation boring you?" Lee asked, not knowing why I suddenly walked away.

"No. It was actually very interesting. Especially because I was a victim in a mass shooting," I replied.

Lee perked up. He and I began discussing the tragic incident that took place at the Route 91 festival. I learned that Lee was no stranger to trauma himself. He was in the military, and his job was to fly Black-hawks, primarily used for casualty evacuation during war. Lee witnessed horrific things throughout his career, and he was now dedicated to helping others heal from trauma and leading the country in security solutions.

"You need to write a book," he said after listening to my story. "You can help people."

He thought it was interesting that after such a traumatic event, I would work in a job that required travel, attendance at large events and going to large cities for conferences.

"Would you be willing to speak at my leadership summit?" he asked.

Remote Security Solutions hosts a yearly Leadership Summit where guest speakers present to industry leaders, widening their knowledge and skills in security solutions. The summit shows companies how to prevent violence and respond when it happens.

Lee, like many people who had been in combat, had a deeper understanding of what I'd been through compared to civilians. People in the military are trained to be shot at. They learn how to run, where to hide and ways to get to safety. They practice these drills.

In Las Vegas, I was in combat. I was being shot at and, without any training at all, had to run to safety. When I share this, there's a shared bond.

"I know if you share what you've been through, it will help our company," he explained. "They need to hear from people they are trying to save. It will help them feel more connected to the work they do."

That encouragement changed the future course of my life.

"Yes! I'll do it!" I said without doubt. By now, I was not only unafraid to speak publicly, I was eager to make myself heard. If Lee thought my story could help people, then I was all in. Seeing my traumatic experience through the lens of post-traumatic growth led me to say *yes* more often.

On the night before the summit, I was nervous. Lee invited me out to dinner so I could process my feelings and ask questions. While we were there, he suggested that I practice.

"Why don't you go ahead and share right now?" Lee said.

"Right now, in the restaurant?" I asked.

"Yes," he said. "Go for it."

I had shared this story over and over again in many different settings. But never to 40 people all at once and never with the agonizing details that Lee wanted me to include. He asked that I make sure I set the scene and described all the obstacles that prevented me from getting to safety sooner.

There were also leaders from big-name companies like Home Depot and Verizon—powerful executives who wanted to learn how to improve the security of both their staff and customers. I sat alongside another trauma survivor who was there to share his story.

I began telling the story of the shooting. As I retold

what happened to me, I knew I had healed so much of my trauma. I wasn't sharing from a place of fear. I wasn't overwhelmed with feelings of trauma.

Sure, I was sad—retelling this story may always bring up difficult emotions for me. But I felt something bigger. By the looks on everyone's faces, I could feel it. *I was helping people.*

I was overwhelmed by the positive response of the audience.

As soon as the applause died down, Lee approached.

"Carly, that was so brave!" he said. "Are you okay?"

"I'm fine," I said, relieved it was over, glad it went so well.

"My CEO was impressed with you!" Lee explained. "As soon as your presentation ended, he leaned over and said, '*Carly just gave us our why!*' I knew that telling your story would make a difference. Thank you!"

By sharing my story publicly, I had motivated the security company to take their work more seriously. After hearing me speak, leadership's commitment to safety grew stronger. They now had a real person—a human face—to represent the incredible work they were doing.

Sharing my story didn't make me weak. It didn't diminish my ability to perform at work or make me seem fragile. I had lived through hell and survived.

"You should do this more often," said the other keynote speaker. "You did an incredible job."

For leaders, this illustrates a crucial principle: strategic vulnerability creates business value. When shared appropriately, personal experiences can inspire teams, strengthen client relationships and differentiate your organization in competitive markets.

The Business Case for Vulnerable Leadership

Showing vulnerability allows employees to connect with leaders on a deeper level. It fosters a sense of relatability and trust, demonstrating they are not alone in challenges they face.

According to *Forbes*, "In the realm of leadership, esteemed researchers have attested to the advantages of embracing vulnerability in improving team culture and performance. The underlying principle is rather straightforward—by embracing vulnerability, leaders create an environment that nurtures trust and opens communication, which are integral components of learning and innovation."[20]

Being vulnerable at work creates trust, promotes team building and streamlines communication. By being a vulnerable leader, I empower my employees to be more open and honest with one another. This breaks down barriers and creates more community.

My friend's dad had a brain aneurysm. He was left

unable to read, write or speak. He had to go on leave from work and use his disability benefits. When it was time for him to return to work, it was clear he was not going to be able to perform in his usual capacity. Luckily, he had supportive and flexible leadership comfortable with vulnerability in the workplace.

Because of this, he was able to be vulnerable and honest with his bosses and admit he simply couldn't do the work, given his brain injury. Leadership stepped in and worked with the team to problem-solve as a group. Some co-workers were able and willing to split his work while he moved into a different department. Most importantly, leadership held his position to ensure he didn't feel penalized or punished for something beyond his control.

If vulnerability had been forbidden, this scenario could have gone very differently. He could've returned to work pretending he could perform—underperforming, missing deadlines and isolating himself from co-workers. The employees, left to pick up the slack, might feel resentful and frustrated.

His performance issues may have led to write-ups and potentially even the loss of his job, leaving the company with a vacant position and the burden of hiring and training someone new. Not only does this affect the bottom line, but it's devastating for team morale and adds unnecessary stress to leadership responsibilities.

Toxic Leadership: The Cost of Invulnerability

Companies without vulnerable leaders often have toxic work cultures. When bosses mistakenly believe vulnerability leads to weakness, lessens power and control and makes them more susceptible to competitors, they often take a stubborn *my way or the highway* approach. CEOs will dictate how the company feels based on how *they* feel, scrutinize anyone who differs and do more long-term damage than they realize.

Unfortunately, I had a leader like this at Grubhub. Our CEO emailed employees, suggesting that anyone who didn't vote like him should resign.

As a manager who respects my employees' legal rights to keep their voting choices confidential, to say I felt uneasy about this would be an understatement. I was put into a position where employees were asking me, "Am I really gonna get fired if I tell you who I voted for?"

I didn't know how to respond. After his comment, I feared making a mistake or saying the wrong thing. This made work feel very stressful. Looking back, I see that so much of how I managed while working there was based on fear of scrutiny or punishment.

It was difficult to have a CEO who made it clear he didn't respect diversity of opinion and thought.

Embracing vulnerability improves flexibility and problem-solving. As a leader, you don't have to know all the answers—and you needn't pretend to. What a relief! You can ask questions, get feedback and implement new plans when you discover old ways are no longer working. It allows for mistakes and a much more fluid —and therefore productive—way of work.

For organizations, the cost of invulnerable leadership is measurable: higher turnover, reduced innovation, decreased employee engagement and increased legal risk from hostile workplace claims. Conversely, vulnerable leadership creates competitive advantages through enhanced team performance, improved retention and stronger customer relationships built on authentic organizational culture.

Implementing Vulnerable Leadership Practices

As a leader, I've always had an open-door policy. Right from the start, I let my employees know I don't judge them for anything. They can talk to me about whatever is going on in their lives or on their mind, and I will listen with respect. I try to model vulnerability by sharing a personal story with my team right away.

I let them know I have kids and a family, and I strive for a work-life balance. I appreciate that they, too, have lives outside of work, and sometimes their personal lives are inseparable from their responsibilities at work. If someone is taking care of an elderly parent or a new baby, I don't expect things to always be perfect. I let them know I trust them to do their best—and to ask for help when they need it.

If I have something I need done, I won't nag employees. I won't email, call and text. I'll find one avenue for sending a message and then let them know they can get back to me when it's convenient. I understand and respect that people have a life outside of work—and I find that respect returns to me when we *are* at work.

Recently, a co-worker needed my help. During a performance review from his previous manager, he was given negative feedback about things he'd done wrong and areas in which they felt he failed.

"Carly, will you look over this with me?" he asked. "I just don't agree with everything they said. I fear that if I go back to them and disagree, I'll be reprimanded."

I looked over the review and saw that, while his supervisors had pointed out what he had done wrong, they failed to offer him any solutions or goals that would help him improve.

"I see why you don't agree with this," I told him. "I would suggest that you email HR, letting them know that you want it to go on the record that you don't agree with what was written." It was clear to me that he only wanted to be heard. "There should be no reprimand for that," I assured him.

As a vulnerable leader, it's my job to listen to what my employees and co-workers need, not to immediately dispute or minimize their concerns. Sometimes just being there for someone can go a long way in helping them develop the right skills and resiliency.

Finally, I show vulnerability by building trust. I do what I say I'm going to do, show up when I'm asked to show up and prove my loyalty to my teams by being an advocate for them. I can't ask them to trust in me if I have yet to prove my trustworthiness to them. This takes time and effort but enhances employee outcomes and loyalty.

Overcoming Barriers to Vulnerability

Not everyone is comfortable with vulnerability. In fact, many trauma survivors are leery of expressing themselves out of fear. Their experience with trauma erodes their sense of safety, and they can become and paranoid.

Others may struggle with vulnerability due to lack of experience. For many, being vulnerable was simply not allowed or acceptable—or was even punished—in their families of origin.

For example, men are often taught to *be strong* or to *suck it up* any time they express feelings of any kind. After years of internalizing this messaging, they no longer feel safe to express themselves.

People may never have had vulnerability modeled to them. They may have grown up in environments with toxic positivity, in which it was not okay to experience—much less to express—negative feelings of any kind. If you've never witnessed someone be vulnerable around you, it can be hard to know what's safe.

I grew up being taught that vulnerability was a weakness. My mom always told me not to cry. She wanted me to show how tough I could be. I didn't want to be seen as a crybaby, so I would suck it up when I felt like crying or being vulnerable.

But shoving down tears rarely works. They came up eventually, and I had to learn to embrace that crying was a way that I expressed emotion.

The first time I cried at DDI, Aaron and Adam were shocked. It was like they'd never seen any emotion in the workplace before.

"What's wrong?" Aaron asked.

"Wh-why are you crying?" Adam asked in disbelief.

"Sometimes I cry, okay?" I explained. "It doesn't mean I'm sad or mad, but that I'm overwhelmed and I'm expressing myself."

Corporate America is often stigmatized as being a place where *feelings* don't belong. Outdated concepts like *leaving home at home*, micromanagement, forced competition and back-to-back meetings, leaving no time for personal life or real self-enrichment, are thankfully losing their lock on management theory.

In fact, a study from the Boise State College of Business and Economics says that "Cultivating an ethical culture is not just about compliance or branding. It is a fundamental pillar for a sustainable, successful business."[21] It goes on to say that embedding ethical practices in management styles leads to significant benefits, including enhanced brand reputation, increased employee satisfaction and sustainable business practices that attract long-term investments.

For leaders, recognizing these barriers allows you to create environments where vulnerability can gradually develop. This might mean starting with small admissions of uncertainty, asking for input on decisions or sharing appropriate personal challenges that demonstrate your humanity without compromising your authority.

Vulnerability Versus Oversharing

It's important to note that *vulnerability* is not the same as *oversharing*.

Vulnerability is a healthy and authentic form of communication. By contrast, *oversharing* means gossip, drama or excessive, manipulative self-revelation in inappropriate contexts.

According to *Pivot*, "Embracing your vulnerability and being able to openly talk about yourself, your life and even deeply personal feelings or events is healthy. However, context is everything. Sharing deeply sensitive information in inappropriate situations or among people who are not ready to offer the corresponding level of intimacy or support might lead you to conclude that your expectations were not realistic."[22]

In other words, *read the room*. Know your audience.

There were times I would share my story, and someone would try to one-up me. They might go into a story about their trauma, feeling like it was the same or even more tragic—even though it may have been very different. I tried not to be offended by this, and I realized that sometimes people do overshare.

This is why it's vital that leaders take a trauma-informed approach. I would never just start telling my story of the shooting without first giving a disclaimer that it contains guns and violence and checking in to make sure it's okay to share. This is just one way a workplace can be more trauma-sensitive.

For leaders, the distinction between vulnerability and oversharing is crucial. Strategic vulnerability involves sharing experiences that serve the team's needs, build trust and model healthy emotional expression. Oversharing, by contrast, burdens employees with inappropriate personal details, creates discomfort and can damage professional relationships.

Building Trauma-Informed Workplaces

Katherine Manning, author of *The Empathetic Workplace*, defines the trauma-informed workplace as an organization that operates with an understanding of trauma and its effects on employees, clients and the communities the company serves, while working to mitigate those effects. She says leaders can do this by providing psychological safety at work.

In an article for *Harvard Business Review*, Manning writes, "Psychological safety is the sense that within a team or organization, it is acceptable for someone to admit that they made a mistake, or don't know the answer, or are struggling. In a recent study, Google found that psychological safety, more than anything else, was critical to making a team work. And the fastest way to build psychological safety was for team members to support each other through hard times." [23]

The way to build this support and safety is to be vulnerable. Leaders who consistently show up as authentic and foster the healthy expression of feelings among employees at work will have better outcomes, employee satisfaction, recruitment and retention—not to mention longer lines of satisfied customers.

My message to employees has always been, *Tell me whatever you need.* As a vulnerable leader, I know it's important that I'm open to communication no matter what the issue.

When Martin was frustrated that I was hired, I listened to him. I didn't negate his feelings, pretend they didn't exist or expect him to get over it. Instead, I listened to his concerns and tried to consider things from his perspective. Because he was open, honest and vulnerable with me, we developed solutions that worked for both of us.

That doesn't mean always giving in to employees or letting them out of challenging situations. I couldn't just give Martin my job. By listening, though, I was able to put my own feelings aside and think creatively about how to handle the situation. The more my employees come and talk to me, the more solutions we can develop together. This promotes psychological safety and a healthy work environment.

Vulnerability as Strategic Courage

Being vulnerable doesn't always mean sharing about hardships or challenges. Sometimes being vulnerable means standing up to a bully. I have had to work with people who didn't have my best interests at heart or who viewed me as a threat instead of a team player. There was a man I worked with who would always put me on the spot during meetings. He'd ask me all kinds of questions that no one would be able to answer without preparation. He was trying to make me look bad.

Instead of retaliating, I prepared. I made sure that before every meeting, I went over my numbers and knew the details of every project. I stayed two steps ahead of him. I documented my concerns, and eventually people figured out what he was doing. I stood up to him by showing my professionalism and being prepared, rather than hiding, avoiding challenges or sinking to his level.

Being vulnerable can also mean being your own cheerleader. It means bringing the team's attention to accomplishments and achievements when they aren't automatically recognized. If no one else is willing to share about your wins, you need to do it yourself. I encourage my employees to share when they close a big client, hit financial targets and meet goals.

Fear can be such a leading factor in whether or not someone is able to be vulnerable at work. When we allow ourselves to be guided by fear, so many negative outcomes can follow.

I love the classic quote, "One thing's for sure, if you don't play, you don't win," from the educator Kylie Francis.

In our professional journeys, many of us face uncertainty and fear failure. But remember: Every chance you don't take is a missed opportunity to learn, grow and succeed.

Whether it's applying for that dream job, speaking up in a meeting or launching a new project, putting yourself out there is the first step toward making an impact. I try to move *toward* fear instead of *away* from it. For me, this includes stepping into my power and owning my success.

For leaders, this represents the highest form of vulnerability: the courage to take calculated risks, advocate for your team and pursue opportunities that could transform your organization.

The Ripple Effect of Authentic Leadership

When my friend Jason Burns asked me to be on his podcast Last2First, I was thrilled. I'd first met Jason at a conference. He was in the courier industry, and his company had recently been acquired by a big-name organization. He was learning so much and told me he wanted to start a podcast.

"I want to share business ideas and get the true stories on how people in this industry get their start," he told me.

His podcast is dedicated to helping leaders uncover success and find ways to grow and succeed. It was an honor that he thought I would be a good fit to speak. In order to do well and help his followers, I had to get vulnerable with myself. I realized my status as an influencer made me a sought-after choice.

People want to hear from me. I'm kind of a big deal.

Each time I take a risk and become vulnerable as a speaker, a leader and a co-worker, I help establish a culture of safety. I enhance the sense of belonging for my employees, and I create an environment that people want to be a part of.

After I was a guest on Jason's podcast, so many of my colleagues and friends reached out congratulating me. Many suggested I speak on more podcasts or panels. I even got sales leads out of it.

All this confirmed that, when I share my experience, I am on the right path.

When sharing my story, I've met countless people who've taken the trouble to thank me. I have put words to some of the feelings they were experiencing. I find this often happens when I talk with people who have served on the police force or those with experience.

I was once telling my story to a gentleman while we were at the ECA conference. He asked what I did for a living, and we talked about our careers.

"I was in the Las Vegas shooting," I explained. "I'm writing a book about the trauma I experienced and how corporations can do a better job of helping their employees who experience trauma."

As he listened, his eyes welled with tears.

"I was in the military. What happened to me while I was in Iraq never really leaves. It's been 12 years, but those memories and trauma are still with me. I can't wait to read your book. I'm so happy you are trying to help people."

By being vulnerable, I made an impact.

For leaders, this illustrates the profound business

value of authentic leadership. When you model vulnerability appropriately, you don't just improve your immediate team dynamics—you create ripple effects that enhance your professional reputation, expand your network and position your organization as a place where people feel genuinely valued and supported.

～

KEY TAKEAWAYS

Vulnerability drives innovation and trust: Teams with psychologically safe environments outperform those led by invulnerable leaders who discourage authentic communication and emotional expression.

Distinguish vulnerability from oversharing: Strategic vulnerability involves appropriate context and timing, while oversharing creates workplace drama and discomfort that damages professional relationships.

Model emotional intelligence: Leaders who demonstrate healthy emotional expression give employees permission to bring their whole selves to work, enhancing engagement and performance.

Create psychological safety frameworks: Establish clear policies and practices that encourage employees to admit mistakes, ask questions and share struggles without fear of retaliation or judgment.

Use trauma-informed communication: Always provide content warnings and check for consent before sharing potentially triggering material in workplace settings to protect vulnerable employees.

Build trust through consistency: Vulnerable leadership requires following through on commitments and demonstrating reliability over time to establish credibility and safety.

Address cultural barriers proactively: Recognize that some employees may have been conditioned to view vulnerability as weakness and provide safe spaces for gradual trust-building.

Leverage vulnerability for business outcomes: Authentic leadership attracts talent, reduces turnover and creates competitive advantages through enhanced team performance, customer loyalty and organizational reputation.

7

BUILDING STRONG SYSTEMS OF ORGANIZATIONAL MENTORSHIP

The email arrived on a Tuesday morning, buried between budget reports and client updates, but its subject line stopped me cold: "Mentorship Program—Would You Be Interested?" I stared at the message from Walmart's leadership development team, reading the invitation to become a mentor in their formal program, and felt a familiar wave of impostor syndrome wash over me.

Me? A mentor? The voice in my head was incredulous. *What could I possibly teach anyone that they couldn't learn better from someone else—someone with more experience, more credentials, more time in leadership roles?*

But even as doubt clouded my initial response, something deeper stirred—a recognition that this opportunity represented the culmination of a journey I hadn't even realized I'd been taking. Somewhere between surviving the Route 91 shooting and rebuilding my professional identity in its aftermath, I had become someone other people sought out for guidance. Colleagues were asking for my perspective on difficult decisions, requesting advice on career moves and confiding struggles they weren't comfortable sharing with their direct supervisors.

When had that shift happened? When had I transformed from someone constantly seeking direction to someone others looked to for answers?

The evolution hadn't been linear or obvious. After the shooting, my outlook had fundamentally changed in ways that took months to fully understand. I found myself constantly scanning for new opportunities—different paths, alternative approaches, possibilities that weren't immediately obvious to everyone else. Having faced mortality at 30, I had developed an urgency about growth and achievement that made me hungry for challenges I would have avoided before.

But hunger without guidance is just restless energy. Without the mentorship I'd received from leaders like Aaron, Adam and Liz—people who had seen potential in me when I couldn't see it myself—that post-trauma drive might have scattered in a dozen different directions, burning bright but achieving little.

Mentors had been the difference between simply surviving my experience and transforming it into professional fuel. They nudged me toward doors I hadn't noticed, showed me paths I hadn't considered and helped me embrace uncertainty when taking new directions felt terrifying. They reminded me, through their words and their faith in my capabilities, that I didn't need to know where every path would lead before I started walking.

Aaron had championed my promotion to vice president of partnerships when I was convinced I wasn't ready for such responsibility. Adam had shown me how to balance professional ambition with personal well-being, modeling the kind of leadership that didn't require sacrificing family for career success. Liz had demonstrated how to command respect in male-dominated environments, teaching me that setting boundaries wasn't aggressive—it was essential.

Each of these mentoring relationships had planted seeds that were now bearing fruit in ways I was only beginning to recognize. The confidence to speak up in board meetings, the ability to advocate for my team during budget negotiations, the willingness to take calculated risks on innovative projects—these capabilities hadn't emerged from formal training programs or leadership seminars. They had grown from the patient investment of people who believed in my potential before I could access it myself.

But here's what struck me as I sat with that mentorship invitation: Before the shooting, I never would have seen myself as someone with valuable insight to share. I understood intellectually that I was one of very few women in senior positions within my industry, but I interpreted that rarity as evidence of my inadequacy rather than recognition of my unique value. I felt like I was constantly playing catch-up, trying to prove I belonged in rooms where I often found myself the only female voice.

The limiting beliefs had been relentless: *I'm too new to this level of responsibility. I don't have enough technical expertise. My perspective isn't as valuable as someone who's been doing this longer.* I measured my worth against male colleagues who had decades of industry experience, concluding that my relative newness meant I had nothing meaningful to contribute to others' development.

After the shooting, those beliefs didn't just gradually fade—they shattered like glass hitting concrete. Trauma has a way of cutting through self-imposed limitations, revealing truths that comfort and routine often obscure. I realized that being a woman in this business wasn't a weakness requiring constant compensation—it was a strength that brought perspectives and insights unavailable to my male colleagues.

My approach to problem-solving, my communication style, my ability to build relationships and navigate complex interpersonal dynamics—these weren't deficiencies to overcome but assets to leverage. The very experiences that had made me feel different and sometimes isolated were exactly what made my mentorship valuable to others facing similar challenges.

When I finally responded to that Walmart email with an enthusiastic "Yes, I'm interested," I wasn't just accepting a role in their mentorship program. I was claiming space as someone whose journey—including its darkest chapters—had created wisdom worth sharing.

For leaders reading this, understand that my transformation from self-doubting employee to confident mentor illustrates a crucial principle that most organizations completely miss: Trauma survivors often become exceptional mentors precisely because of their experiences, not despite them. The same qualities that help people navigate profound personal challenges—resilience, emotional intelligence, the ability to find meaning in difficulty, comfort with uncertainty—are exactly the qualities that make someone capable of guiding others through professional and personal growth.

Yet most companies fail to recognize this connection. They see employees returning from trauma as problems to manage rather than resources to leverage. They focus on accommodating limitations rather than identifying new capabilities. They provide support for healing without considering how that healing might create unprecedented value for organizational development.

This represents one of the most significant missed opportunities in modern talent management. Organizations that can identify and leverage the natural mentoring capabilities that often emerge from traumatic experiences gain access to a competitive advantage that can't be replicated through traditional training programs or external consulting.

Because here's what I discovered through my own mentoring relationships and in the years I've spent developing others: The most powerful mentorship doesn't come from people who've had easy paths to success. It comes from those who've faced genuine adversity, processed it constructively and emerged with hard-won wisdom about resilience, adaptation and growth.

The mentor who can say "I've been where you are, and I know the way through" carries credibility that no amount of theoretical knowledge can match. The leader who has navigated their own season of uncertainty can guide others through similar territory with empathy and practical insight. The executive who has transformed personal trauma into professional strength becomes uniquely qualified to help others find meaning and purpose in their own difficult experiences.

But this transformation from survivor to mentor doesn't happen automatically. It requires intentional development, strategic support and organizational cultures that recognize the connection between personal growth and professional value. It demands leaders who can see beyond immediate performance metrics to identify employees whose life experiences have created mentoring capabilities worth cultivating.

In the pages that follow, you'll discover how to build mentorship systems that capture this untapped potential, how to identify employees whose personal journeys have prepared them for exceptional mentoring roles and how to create organizational cultures where trauma survivors become developmental assets rather than accommodation challenges.

You'll learn practical frameworks for pairing mentors and mentees strategically, approaches for supporting trauma-informed mentoring relationships and methods for measuring the business impact of mentorship programs that tap into the wisdom born from adversity. Most importantly, you'll understand how organizations that master these approaches don't just support individual healing—they transform personal pain into competitive advantage.

Because sometimes, all it takes to recognize new opportunities in your career or your life is for someone to show you a different door, path or possibility you hadn't considered. And sometimes, the people best qualified to point toward those opportunities are those who've walked through the darkest doors themselves and emerged with maps others can follow.

The question isn't whether your organization has employees with mentoring potential born from difficult experiences—it does. The question is whether you can recognize that potential and create systems sophisticated enough to transform individual survival into organizational strength.

From Self-Doubt to Strategic Advantage

The road to leadership wasn't always easy. Even before the shooting, my career was full of challenges I had to overcome. There were many times that I encountered naysayers—people who told me that I can't do something or that I don't know enough.

I've always been told, *You have a lot to learn, Carly.* Mostly by men.

There were times when these comments could make me feel small or unworthy. But after the shooting, I saw them as fuel for transformation. If someone thought I couldn't do something, I wanted to prove them wrong. I wanted to show the naysayers what I was capable of.

One year, after a big conference, an executive called me out of the blue. "Carly," he said, "I just want you to know that you have so much to learn. You're new to this space, and you need to learn who the big players are and how to handle yourself."

Despite his rudeness, I listened closely. He was right

about one thing: I *did* have a lot to learn! Thanks to his feedback, I accepted the challenge. I would learn everything I needed to in order to be successful. I was driven to become one of these "big players," and I would do whatever it took to get there.

But people didn't always take me seriously. One time, I got a call from a CEO. He wanted to partner with DDI, but before hashing out the details, he asked to "speak with my manager." Because I was a woman, he didn't think I could be trusted with my authority.

I put him through to my managers, who gently explained to him that I was the lead on this particular sale. "Whatever Carly says is how the deal will go down," Aaron explained. "She's the lead on this."

Knowing Aaron had my back was a mark of his success as a mentor. He empowered me to stand my ground and have confidence in myself, knowing I wasn't alone.

At first, I struggled with confidence. Continuously being told that I had a lot to learn didn't help. When I walked into a room, I wasn't sure if I was smart enough or had the right ideas. I questioned myself. I needed reassurance.

But being shot at and running for my life really changed the way I view challenges. I witnessed a horrible mass shooting and I lived to tell the tale. Nothing about the experience was easy—and it empowered me to do other hard things and take on new challenges. Now, I felt unstoppable.

For organizations, this transformation represents exactly the kind of leadership development that formal mentorship programs can accelerate. When employees receive proper support through challenges, they don't just survive—they become leaders who can guide others through similar difficulties.

Learning from Exceptional Mentors

Among my mentors, Adam, Aaron and Liz stand out. Adam helped me learn how to balance my work life and my personal life. When I started at DDI, he was new to fatherhood—and he knew the specific challenges a new parent can face. He always supported me and helped me grow not just as a worker and leader, but as a person.

Of everyone who's supported me, Aaron has always had my back no matter what. He could see that, by helping me succeed, he helped the company succeed. He encouraged me to seize opportunities and develop as a leader. He knew I was loyal and hardworking, and he saw that, after everything I'd been through, my career became my passion.

Liz was my first female mentor. I met her through the ECA board. She showed me how to handle myself as a female in a male-dominated industry. Watching her in meetings and seeing who she was as a leader shaped who I wanted to become—someone who trusted her judgment and refused to back down when she knew she was right.

Of all my powerful moments with Liz, one meeting stands out. She was sharing one of her ideas when a male colleague interrupted her, ostensibly to move the meeting along.

"Excuse me," Liz said, without flinching. "I'm not done speaking."

Whoa, I thought. *So, that's how you do it.*

Up to that point, I'd been interrupted so many times in so many meetings that I had come to accept it. Men talked over me or down to me and often disregarded what I was saying entirely. Watching Liz gave me the courage to trust myself and do the same.

Shortly after working with Liz, I faced yet another hard situation. In an important board meeting, a male colleague became frustrated with me. He spoke to me in a demeaning tone. He interrupted me and said, "Carly, you're not hearing me."

I felt belittled. But I'd seen how Liz handled herself, set boundaries and calmly refused to back down.

I used her approach. "I am hearing you," I said, then repeated his criticism back to him. "This isn't the time for an argument," I stated, and moved the meeting forward.

Thanks to having a strong mentor, I stood up for

myself and set a boundary. I let it be known that this sort of behavior was unacceptable. And he has never spoken to me like that again.

I wanted—*needed*—to give that gift of strength to others. I knew that through mentoring, I could be that person for someone else. I could share the knowledge and experience I've gained to help others find their passions and gain courage to go for their big dreams.

For leaders, this illustrates the multiplier effect of effective mentorship. One strong mentor doesn't just develop one person—they create leaders who go on to develop others, creating exponential returns on mentorship investments.

Strategic Mentoring in Action

One of my first mentees was a woman who had trouble setting boundaries. She was new to the industry and didn't trust that she had the authority to stand up for herself. Her co-workers took control of her calendar and scheduled meetings at all hours of the day—some in the middle of the night.

When I met her, she was terribly stressed. For starters, she was sleep-deprived, which makes everything twice as hard. She was also having trouble holding any sort of relationship outside of work.

I explained to her that she had to set boundaries. "You have the right to block off your schedule so no one can schedule a meeting," I explained. "If they schedule one anyway, you have the right to decline. Not everyone deserves your time. You can set limits. You must."

"Won't I get fired if I say *no* to people?" she asked. She didn't believe she could set limits and boundaries.

"What? No!" I explained. "If a CEO wants to see you, you might want to make time. But you also need to block off time on your calendar when you aren't working. Let everyone know your calendar is up to date, and if a time is blocked, it means you're not available. End of story."

All she needed was someone who had her back and gave her the confidence to stand her ground.

At our next meeting, she was so much happier. "My relationship with my boyfriend has never been better," she said. "Thanks to you, I'm finally setting boundaries, and things already feel so much more balanced."

Another mentee was frustrated because no one recognized her work. Her colleagues openly took advantage of her and piled more work on her desk— because they knew she would get it done.

I encouraged her to showcase her work in a more powerful light and become her own cheerleader. "Before they recognize you, you have to recognize yourself," I explained. "Ask for time in a meeting to showcase your work and give yourself accolades for your accomplishments."

"Really?" she asked incredulously.

"Who *else* will do it?" I replied. "Everyone is so busy. They don't know you like you know yourself. How could they? You have to make space and time to be seen."

A few months later, she was recognized by the company and got the lead on a major project.

For organizations, these examples demonstrate the ROI of mentorship programs. Both mentees became more effective employees, more confident leaders and stronger contributors to their teams. The investment in mentorship time paid dividends in improved performance and retention.

The Business Case for Formal Mentorship Programs

Mentor/mentee relationships can provide significant benefits in the workplace. According to LinkedIn, "By establishing a formal mentoring program, businesses can create a better working culture that fosters learning and growth for their employees."[24] It lists benefits to the mentee, including increased self-confidence, enhanced self-awareness, job satisfaction, more bold career aspirations, better likelihood of promotions, greater loyalty to companies and greater personal fulfillment.

Mentors build confidence and help mentees find their unique talents. A mentor can acknowledge and validate a mentee on a more personal, meaningful level than a boss can.

For example, I had an employee who wanted to quit. I saw she was a talented and highly skilled employee. She was too good to let go. I reached out to her to determine her needs and helped create a position for her that helped her develop her talents. Before I knew it, she'd worked her way up to a senior management position. She was a huge asset to the company—she just needed to see it herself.

A mentor/mentee relationship can also be a key to more effective networking, which can help individuals and organizations ideate, collaborate and recognize opportunities.

For trauma survivors, having understanding mentorship at work can make a world of difference. As someone who has gone through trauma, I'm often drawn to people who have experienced challenges. I know that they may need special encouragement and support from someone who can empathize.

Trauma-Informed Mentoring Practices

Recently, I was on my way to a big meeting with Sean. When we got to the airport, Sean confessed that he was in a lot of pain.

"Why are you here?" I asked. "You need to get checked out by medical professionals."

"Carly, I can't miss this meeting," he said. "It's a huge opportunity."

"Yes, you can!" I explained. "No opportunity is *that* huge. Your health matters and you need to go find out what's wrong."

I've been a mentor to Sean for a long time, which made me uniquely qualified to help him recognize his blind spots. He was putting his work before his health. I helped him see that, by not taking care of himself, he wasn't solving problems. He was creating them.

He ended up going to the hospital and learned that he had serious issues with his spine that needed immediate attention. Traveling on an airplane could've made things much worse for him.

Having been through trauma, I give people more grace. I can sense when something is wrong, and I'm not afraid to ask what's going on. I know how to offer help and resources because I know that sometimes the easiest thing—like showing up for a meeting—can feel unmanageable.

One time, an employee who I knew had been struggling reached out and asked me to take over one of his tasks. He needed me to purchase something for a client.

"I just can't order this stuff right now," he said, feeling defeated.

"Sure! No problem," I said.

This wasn't something he'd asked of me before, so I knew this time was different. I knew he needed me. I didn't ask questions or judge him. I simply placed the order when he clearly couldn't. I'd been in similar straits myself, and I could empathize with his needs.

According to the Lyda Hill Institute for Human Resilience, "The heart of trauma-informed mentorship lies in the concept of building trusting and supportive relationships. Mentors serve as beacons of hope, offering survivors a safe space to share their needs, dreams and goals. Through these relationships, survivors begin the journey of healing, reclaiming their lives and envisioning a future filled with possibilities." [25]

One of the most important things I do when I'm mentoring someone is one of the simplest: to be there for them. To make time for them. To commit to supporting them—and follow through. I check in and let them know that, even if it seems like the whole world is against them, *I care.*

For leaders, this approach creates measurable value. Employees who feel supported through difficulties are more likely to stay with the organization, perform at higher levels and become loyal advocates for the company culture.

Building Gender-Inclusive Mentorship Systems

As one of the few females in my industry, it's important for me to find ways to mentor women in particular. A few years ago, my mentor Liz saw the need for more women's voices in our profession. She petitioned the ECA board to develop a women's committee focused solely on giving women more power in the transportation industry—and making sure they knew how to use it.

It wasn't easy! The board, which was overwhelmingly male, didn't immediately see why this mattered. They felt that we had everything covered in our other committees. The need for providing specific support to talented, ambitious women wasn't something they particularly valued. The women on the board had to fight to get approval—which meant refusing to accept *no* as an answer.

Now, the ECA board has its own committee dedicated solely to women and women's development, education, leadership and more. It's focused on increasing skills so women gain confidence in their roles and learn how to navigate their careers.

We host an educational webinar series in which women in leadership roles speak and share their experience and knowledge. It motivates the women in the room to keep going, growing and learning—and to know when (and how) to stand their ground. We plan to develop a mentorship program as well.

Carrie Ehlers was the ECA board's first female president. Having a female as a board president in this industry was rare. She was an inspiration to many women who wanted seats at the table. Sadly, she passed away from cancer while in the president role. The board formed a scholarship fund for women in business, cementing her grand legacy of mentorship.

For organizations, this demonstrates the strategic importance of targeted mentorship programs. Gender-specific and diversity-focused mentoring initiatives don't just support individual employees—they strengthen entire talent pipelines and improve organizational culture.

The Mutual Benefits of Strategic Mentorship

But it's not just the mentee that benefits from this kind of relationship. There are many benefits to the mentor as well. According to *The Chronicle of Evidence-Based Mentoring*, being a mentor is an opportunity to continue to learn and grow.[26] Mentors can look back on lessons learned and gain perspective. They might even learn something new!

Mentoring has helped me in so many ways. When I see a mentee is succeeding, I know I'm succeeding. And I *want* to see people succeed. It's fulfilling to see people grow, and there's always more room at the top. When I see someone who trusts me thrive, it gives me a greater sense of purpose.

Aaron often told me how he felt good about helping people put food on the table, creating more jobs and more opportunities and opening doors for others—not just professionally, but personally too.

When I help someone grow, they may get a raise, which they can use to buy a car or an engagement ring they've been saving up for. Their whole life can improve —and what's more exciting than that? I want to be a part of it. It drives me to do better. It helps me give back.

For organizations, this reciprocal value creation strengthens employee engagement, builds internal networks and creates cultures where people genuinely want to help each other succeed.

Building Resilience Through Mentorship

Since the shooting, I've found that things that used to feel scary at work, like asking for a promotion, giving a speech or doing a presentation, just aren't scary anymore. My threshold for fear is different now. Where once I was weak and uncertain, I am now strong and resilient.

Fortunately, you don't need to survive a mass shooting to increase your tolerance for stress. I help mentees see that they can work with their own stress and fear to grow resilience.

According to *Psychology Today*, "A common theme underlying most anxiety is discomfort with or fear of uncertainty. The more uncomfortable you are with uncertainty, the more likely you are to struggle with anxiety."[27]

Uncertainty is inescapable and it's up to us to recognize it, embrace it and work with it, not against it.

I love to ask big, scary questions. *What if...? What's the worst that could happen?*

The article goes on to explain that there are ways to grow your tolerance for uncertainty. Things like shifting the focus from *what if* to *even if* can remind you that you have the ability to cope, no matter the outcome.

Instead of focusing on all that could go wrong, I encourage my mentees to focus on what they might gain by taking risks. Taking a risk means you might not succeed—at least, not the first time. I help my mentees see how what they consider failure can lead to growth.

For leaders, this resilience-building approach creates employees who are more innovative, adaptable and capable of handling challenging situations— exactly the kind of workforce needed to thrive in uncertain business environments.

Scaling Mentorship Across Organizations

Not every mentor has to be a boss or someone working in your field. When I was new to Walmart, I wanted to learn from the senior VP at the time. She was a woman I could tell had unique wisdom to offer. Even though we weren't directly connected, I took a risk and reached out.

"Hey, can I just have a quick 15 minutes of your time?" I asked. "I have a lot to learn, and I'd love to pick your brain."

We talked and she shared so much life-changing knowledge. At the end of our talk, I said, "If you're ever willing to take on a mentee, I'd love to learn more from you."

She was more than happy to meet with me and offer me guidance and support.

My dad was my first mentor—and one of the greatest. He lived by the phrase *It doesn't hurt to ask*.

"But what if they yell at me?" I asked jokingly.

"Then they yell at you," he laughed.

Today, I'm not too scared to ask for what I want. In fact, I wouldn't be where I am today if I didn't put myself out there, seek out people I knew had something to offer and keep going in the face of challenge or uncertainty.

For organizations, this demonstrates the importance of creating cultures where mentorship requests are welcomed and encouraged. When employees feel comfortable seeking guidance from leaders at all levels, knowledge transfer accelerates and innovation flourishes.

The most successful mentorship programs aren't just formal structures—they're cultural shifts that make every interaction an opportunity for growth and development. Leaders who embrace this approach don't just develop individual employees—they transform entire organizational capabilities.

~

KEY TAKEAWAYS

Formalize mentorship as strategic investment: Organizations with structured mentorship programs see higher employee retention, faster skill development and improved succession planning that directly impacts bottom-line results.

Identify trauma-informed mentoring opportunities: Employees who've overcome significant challenges often make exceptional mentors for others facing difficulties, creating unique competitive advantages in talent development.

Create cross-functional mentoring relationships: Pair employees from different departments and levels to build organizational knowledge, break down silos and accelerate innovation.

Address gender and diversity gaps systematically: Establish specific mentoring programs for underrepresented groups to accelerate leadership development and strengthen talent pipelines.

Measure mentorship outcomes: Track metrics like promotion rates, engagement scores and retention among mentored employees to demonstrate ROI and refine program effectiveness.

Encourage reverse mentoring: Younger employees can mentor senior staff on technology and cultural trends while receiving career guidance in return, creating mutual value.

Build resilience through shared vulnerability: Mentors who can discuss overcoming challenges help mentees develop higher risk tolerance and stress management skills crucial for leadership roles.

Scale mentorship beyond formal programs: Encourage informal mentoring relationships and provide training for employees to recognize mentoring opportunities in daily interactions, creating cultures of continuous development.

8

CRISIS AND GENDER: THE TEND-AND-BEFRIEND ADVANTAGE

The questions started almost immediately after we returned from Las Vegas, spilling out of me like water from a broken dam. I couldn't stop asking Kevin about details, seeking confirmation for memories that felt too surreal to trust. We'd sit at the kitchen table over morning coffee, and I'd launch into the same litany of confusion and disbelief that had been cycling through my mind since that terrible night.

"Why didn't that man get up and run when everyone else was screaming?" I'd ask for the 10th time, my voice urgent with the need to understand. "Why did the woman beside us fall down? Was she shot or did she trip? Did you see that security guard too—the one pointing toward the exit like we were leaving a routine event? Did he really not notice a shooting was going on?"

The questions tumbled out faster than Kevin could answer them, each one carrying the weight of my desperate attempt to make sense of an experience that had shattered every assumption I'd held about safety, predictability and the basic order of the world. I needed to know that what I remembered was real, that the chaos and terror weren't products of my traumatized imagination but actual events witnessed by someone else I trusted.

Kevin would patiently answer each question, providing the confirmation and validation I craved. Yes, he'd seen the man who couldn't seem to move. Yes, the woman had fallen—whether from a bullet or from being trampled, neither of us could say for certain. Yes, that security guard had seemed completely oblivious to the magnitude of what was unfolding around him. Kevin's memories matched mine, proving I wasn't losing my grip on reality—it really had been as horrific and confusing as I remembered.

But here's what struck me as profoundly strange: Kevin had very little to say about the night beyond answering my questions. He was willing to engage with my need to process, supportive of my endless verbal examination of every detail, but he didn't seem to *need* to talk about it the way I did. He wasn't compelled to relive the event through conversation, to dissect every moment, to search for meaning in the madness.

For Kevin, the experience seemed to exist in a different category entirely—something that had happened, been survived and could now be filed away. When I asked him how he was handling the trauma, he looked genuinely puzzled by the question. He was heartbroken and deeply saddened by the tragedy, certainly. The loss of life affected him profoundly. But he wasn't *traumatized* in the way I understood the term —he wasn't reliving it, wasn't hypervigilant, wasn't struggling with intrusive thoughts and memories.

"I was hyper-focused on one thing," he explained when I pressed him about his experience. "I've got to get my wife to safety. That's all I could think about. Once we made it to the hotel room, once we were safe—that was it. The threat was over."

His matter-of-fact delivery revealed something I was only beginning to understand: We had experienced the same event but processed it through completely different neural pathways, different emotional frameworks, different biological and social programming. While I was drowning in the need to verbally process and make meaning from chaos, Kevin had compartmentalized the experience as a problem that had been solved successfully.

Throughout his life, Kevin had enjoyed playing paintball—a competitive team shooting sport that had trained him to think tactically under pressure. In paint-ball, you're constantly scanning for threats, planning escape routes, anticipating obstacles and making split-second decisions about movement and safety. When the gunfire started that night, these skills rose to the surface automatically. He looked over the chaotic scene, and his mind immediately shifted into strategic mode: *What's my next obstacle? What's the safest path? How do I get us out of here?*

I had no equivalent experience to draw from. I'd never been in a situation that required tactical thinking under extreme pressure, never trained to suppress panic in favor of strategic action. When the shooting started, I froze—my mind desperately trying to process what sounds I was hearing, what was happening around us, what it all meant. While Kevin was already planning our escape route, I was still trying to under-stand whether we were actually in danger.

It was Kevin's decisiveness that saved us. He grabbed my hand and pulled me through obstacles I might not have seen, guided me around bottlenecks I couldn't have anticipated, made choices about direction and timing that my panicked brain couldn't have calcu-lated. His ability to suppress emotional processing in favor of immediate action got us to safety.

Once we reached our hotel room, I could sense Kevin's profound relief—not just that we had survived, but that his mission was complete. He had successfully protected the person he loved most. The problem had been identified, addressed and resolved. For him, the crisis was over.

For me, the crisis was just beginning. While Kevin could file the experience away as a successfully navigated emergency, I needed to understand it, integrate it, find meaning in it. I needed to talk it through until the experience made sense, until I could reconcile what had happened with my understanding of how the world was supposed to work.

This fundamental difference in our responses puzzled me initially. Were we just wired differently as individuals? Was this about personality, background or something deeper? It took months of research and therapy to understand that what I was witnessing wasn't unique to Kevin and me—it was a pattern that scientists have been documenting across gender lines for decades.

For leaders reading this, understanding these profoundly different responses to crises isn't just personal curiosity—it's strategic intelligence that can transform how organizations support employees through trauma and leverage diverse strengths during challenging times. The same biological and social factors that shaped Kevin's tactical response and my verbal processing drive workplace behaviors in ways that most managers completely misunderstand.

When a crisis hits your organization—whether it's a

traumatic event, market upheaval, leadership transition or operational emergency—your employees will respond through the same gendered patterns that Kevin and I demonstrated that night. Some will immediately shift into action mode, focusing on solutions, next steps and tactical responses. Others will need to process, discuss, seek understanding and build consensus before they can move forward effectively.

Most organizations treat these different responses as better or worse, more professional or less professional, more leadership-worthy or more needy. They reward the quick action-takers and struggle to accommodate the processors. They interpret immediate tactical thinking as strength and verbal processing as weakness. They design crisis response systems around fight-or-flight mentalities while completely missing the strategic value of tend-and-befriend approaches.

This represents one of the most significant missed opportunities in modern crisis management. Research shows that the most resilient organizations aren't those that rely on single response patterns—they're those that can harness both immediate tactical action and longer-term community-building approaches. They understand that the employees who seem to "fall apart" during initial crisis phases often become the ones who hold teams together during extended difficult periods.

In the pages that follow, you'll discover how these gendered crisis responses evolved, why they both have strategic value and how smart organizations can design support systems that accommodate different processing styles while maximizing collective resilience. You'll learn to recognize the signs of tend-and-befriend responses versus fight-or-flight patterns, understand how cultural expectations amplify or suppress natural stress responses and implement leadership strategies that leverage both approaches.

Most importantly, you'll understand why the future of organizational resilience depends not on choosing between these response patterns, but on creating environments where both can flourish and complement each other. Because the same crisis that reveals Kevin's tactical leadership capabilities also reveals my community-building strengths—and organizations that can harness both will outperform those that rely on only one approach.

The question isn't whether your employees will respond to crisis differently based on their gender, background and socialization—they will. The question is whether your organization can create systems sophisticated enough to support all those response patterns and strategic enough to leverage them for competitive advantage.

Because sometimes the person who needs to talk through every detail isn't processing trauma—they're building the understanding and consensus that will hold your team together long after the immediate crisis has passed. And sometimes the person who seems unaffected by traumatic events isn't callous—they're maintaining the calm, tactical thinking that will guide your organization to safety.

Both responses are gifts. The leaders who learn to recognize and cultivate both will build the most resilient organizations of the future.

Understanding Gender Differences in Crisis Responses

The differences in how Kevin and I processed our shared experience could be a function of our very different personalities, but research suggests deeper biological and social factors may also be at play. According to a study from Brigham Young University examining how men and women experience walking home at night differently, "Women focused significantly more on potential safety hazards—the periphery of the images—while men looked directly at focal points or their intended destination."[28]

In other words, men didn't have to worry that there might be a threat nearby. They didn't scan their surroundings, increase their pace or look behind them to make sure they weren't being followed. As a group, fear simply wasn't as prevalent for men as it was for women.

An article analyzing gender differences in stress

responses describes a study finding that, when it comes to stress, men and women might react differently due to biological factors.

"Women typically have a higher level of oxytocin combined with estrogen, which influences a tend-and-befriend response to stress. Men, influenced by testosterone, often lean toward a fight-or-flight response. Research also shows variabilities in the hippocampus and amygdala among genders, which further explains why stress triggers and responses can differ vastly between men and women."[29]

When faced with trauma, men are more likely to experience a fight-or-flight response—an instinctual psychological reaction to a threatening situation. When overcome with a fight-or-flight response, a person prepares to either forcibly resist an oncoming threat or run away. At the first sounds of gunshots, Kevin jumped into fight-or-flight mode while I stood frozen.

Women are more likely to engage in the tend-and-befriend response to stress. Rather than directly challenging a threat, the tend-and-befriend response involves tending to your loved ones by pulling them close, physically or figuratively.

The tend-and-befriend theory, developed by social psychologist Shelley Taylor, says that humans may seek social support and connection when facing a threat. If these social connections strengthened by tend-and-befriend behaviors are healthy, then women can find themselves healing through social support and connectedness. Men might feel a sense of relief after successfully defending themselves or escaping from a threat.

In other words, Kevin didn't feel the need to cope by talking it out or ruminating over the details of what happened that night. For him, once we made it to safety, the threat was gone and the danger was eliminated. He could move on. I, however, really wanted to talk about what happened and sought as much social connection as I could to do so.

For leaders, recognizing these different stress responses enables more effective crisis management. Teams with diverse gender representation can leverage both immediate action-oriented responses and longer-term community-building approaches to organizational challenges.

The Cultural Construction of Gender Responses

According to *Psychology Today*, "From an early age, men are socialized to believe that their worth is something they must build through achievement, status and financial security. Unlike women, who are often valued for their youth and beauty, men are rarely considered 'desirable' in their younger years unless they have already amassed resources, power or social influence." [30]

This makes it harder for men to be vulnerable, share feelings and process emotions. Instead, they often focus on external accomplishments to maintain the perception of being successful and worthy. When men feel stressed or emotional, it might lead to uncomfortable feelings of inadequacy and weakness.

According to a study done by the online therapy company Talkspace, "Societal expectations and stigmas that exist around mental health prevent some men from even acknowledging they feel stressed at all—and seeking help is out of the question. After all, we live in a culture that promotes toughness in males, which leaves some stressed men resigned to endure pain on their own."[31]

The industry I work in is male-dominated. It's not that men don't feel emotions at work, because they do. It's just that they express them differently. In a LinkedIn article called "Why There's No Room for Women's Emotions in the Workplace," the author explains, "If you look closely, you'll find that the acceptable emotions (for men) are predominantly at the negative end of the spectrum. The emotions you'll encounter are anger, aggression, ridicule, frustration, cynicism or schadenfreude."[32]

When I first cried in front of Aaron and Adam at work, it was clear they were uncomfortable. They thought crying was what happened when someone felt sad. It's true that I cried when I was sad, but also when I had other feelings, like feeling overwhelmed or angry. For me, crying was a healthy way to express my feelings. But they thought something was wrong.

For leaders, understanding these cultural constraints enables more inclusive approaches to emotional expression and stress management that benefit all employees regardless of gender.

The Leadership Stress Epidemic

Regardless of the differences in how men and women experience and manage stress and trauma, research shows that most modern leaders feel stressed by the demands of their jobs. According to *Entrepreneur*, 71 percent of those in management positions feel "mounting pressures of digital transformation, economic uncertainty and evolving workplace dynamics [which] have created a perfect storm of leadership stress that demands immediate attention and strategic intervention."[33]

The article continues: "Leaders cast long shadows across their organizations, with their behaviors and emotional states reverberating through every level of the company. Their influence on organizational cultures is profound and far-reaching, as employees naturally look to their leaders as behavioral role models."

Many of the male leaders I've worked with were

stressed due to the high demands of their jobs. Each handled stress differently. Some shut down in the face of stress—closing their door, not responding to emails, canceling meetings and ghosting staff. Some focused solely on actions that would alleviate their current stress, which was problematic because much of their stress didn't affect *all* employees. As a result, employees felt overlooked and undervalued.

For organizations, this creates a cascade effect where leadership stress becomes institutionalized, impacting collective performance and innovation capacity. Understanding gender-based stress responses helps leaders develop more effective coping strategies that benefit entire teams.

Developing Gender-Informed Leadership Strategies

As a female leader who has also experienced trauma, managing stress is high on my priority list. I've dealt with a lot over the years—the shooting, the death of my dad and living through a pandemic. Learning healthy coping mechanisms was essential. I didn't want my stress to trickle down to the team I was leading.

In addition to open, free-flowing communication, one of the most effective things I do to manage stress is to run. Running has helped me take a beat before reacting to my feelings in outsized or destructive ways. If there's something stressing me out, before I deal with it, I go for a run, clear my head and find more clarity before developing a solution.

I've worked with many leaders over the years who struggled to manage their stress. Instead, when a stressor surfaced, they reacted. Sometimes, this meant making unnecessary, counterproductive or impulsive decisions that affected entire teams. As a leader who has faced trauma, I know the repercussions that sweeping changes can make, especially for employees who are going through personal trauma or struggles.

As a female leader who is comfortable with my wide range of emotions, I've learned not to make rash and impulsive decisions. I take time to think things through and remind myself to look at the bigger picture. I ask myself, *What is the real effect of this problem? Is it affecting one percent of the company or 80 percent?*

If it's only affecting one percent of the company, then there's maybe only a small group that needs a tweak or change. I can make that change by working with each individual in a one-on-one meeting, taking the time to explain what is happening and why, rather than sending a blast email to the entire organization.

I have the philosophy that not every problem is a fire that needs to be immediately extinguished. By living through such a traumatic event, I've found that I'm not easily shaken by typical workplace stressors. I've trained myself to hold back quick reactions to stressors and instead clearly process the situation and develop intentional plans.

Emphasizing Process-Driven Solutions

Another way I manage stress is to intentionally develop processes. Lack of process is a huge trigger to stress. When you plan for stress and trauma, it's more easily managed. Stress and trauma are going to come up in business, whether we like it or not.

Developing a process for handling problems at work is such an easy way to keep additional stressors at bay. When problems arise and there is no plan or procedure in place, the entire team feels the effects. Process equals accountability. It decreases confusion and finger-pointing and helps provide staff with the clarity they need.

When I first started at DDI, Aaron told me that I needed to remove a driver from our platform for performance and safety issues.

"Okay," I said. "What are the steps for this? What's the process?"

"You're in charge of that now," Aaron explained. "We don't have a process in place for something like this."

I got right to work. Having processes in place shows employees you care. Everyone deserves to know and understand the policies and procedures that apply to their lives. I developed a process for exiting drivers from our platform that was clear and easily delivered.

It's easy for a stressed-out leader to see a problem and reach for a quick fix or put a Band-Aid on the situation. But bandages can't always heal a wound by themselves. You can't put a Band-Aid on a bullet hole.

In other words, if there is no process in place, then a quick fix won't solve anything in the long term. Even though time is of the essence when making decisions during an emergency, the most important thing a leader can do is to step back, evaluate the procedures and make wider, more sustainable changes.

I recently had a situation with a staff member who needed more than a bandage or quick fix. We were making changes within the organization, particularly with staffing. My employee was asked to meet with a very important customer to close a big deal, but felt that he didn't understand the customers and their needs or how we could help.

"Carly, can we connect?" he asked.

"Of course," I responded.

"I don't feel like I have all the information on this client. I don't want to look like a fool," he stressed.

"I hear you," I said. "Let's make a plan."

I helped him take a step back and get the right people in the room. He gathered the necessary information from those who knew the customer best and was able to get a better idea of the customer's needs. More importantly, I impressed on him the importance of honesty, clarity and respect.

"We need to tell the client we haven't yet learned everything we need to know about his company," I explained. "Let him know we're working on it, and that it's important to us to get it right. We need to be honest *and* reassuring. Let him know we've got this."

By pretending to know the client and rushing into the meeting unprepared, we may have made a mistake that could've felt inauthentic or dismissive. Instead, we took a step back to re-evaluate what else could be done. This lowered my employee's stress and gave us an opportunity to meet the client's needs more effectively.

Strategic Planning for Stress Reduction

Another way I handle stress as a leader is by having yearly planning meetings focused on goals and strategies. I like to work with my teams to talk things out. We go over what goals we met and how we were successful. We also discuss stressors and how we might handle those differently.

Our leadership team comes together to look over progress of the company and listen to the needs of those employees working on the front lines. We ask questions like, *Did our plans go as followed? What were our strengths? Where did we fail?*

I like to use a strategy called "Start, Stop and Continue." As a team, we look over the successes and failures of the past year.

For "**Start**": We determine what we need to *start* doing. *Is there something we haven't done that could have a positive return on investment? Is there a tool that could make things easier?*

For "**Stop**": Is there something we need to *stop* doing? *Were there plans in place that weren't effective or caused more stress than necessary?*

For "**Continue**": *What worked really well that we want to continue?* This is a great place to acknowledge team members who worked hard and contributed, and focus on the positive.

This process reduces stress and sets us up for success. Yes, it takes time. But it's an intentional step that will be effective in reducing overall stress. When leaders reduce their own stress, the company as a whole feels supported.

Leveraging Gender-Based Leadership Strengths

Both female and male leaders have strengths and weaknesses when it comes to stress and management style. According to *Managers Lab*, "Women leaders tend to use a transformational leadership approach, working with employees to set common goals and achieve them together. On the other hand, leading men often resort to transactional leadership, exchanging rewards for employee performance. In addition, an analysis of studies on women's and men's leadership indicates that women leaders are perceived as more democratic, participatory and inclusive."[34]

I feel fortunate that over my career, I've found the strategies that make me a better leader. When I express my emotions effectively, I'm more grounded and easier to work with. When I apply the necessary policies and procedures, everyone is clear on expectations. When I use proactive approaches to stress, I make better decisions and don't react with impulse.

All of these strategies keep me connected to the work I'm doing and, most importantly, to my team. Connection is a key component of a healthy and thriving management style.

For organizations, the most effective approach combines both transformational and transactional leadership styles, leveraging the strengths that different leaders bring based on their experiences, gender socialization and natural tendencies.

Building Gender-Inclusive Support Systems

It's impossible to describe what it was like to be at the shooting on that terrible night. The sounds of the gunshots sounded like fireworks. The sight of bodies dropping is indescribable. The screams of terror still ring in my ears. The feeling of confusion when stuck in a stampede was suffocating.

There was a group of women I knew who attended the concert together—without their husbands or boyfriends. When they went home and tried to describe what had happened, they found it practically impossible. While their loved ones had sympathy for what happened to them, they didn't have empathy. It's nearly impossible to understand and relate to this kind of experience if you haven't lived through it yourself.

Even if their partners were there, I wonder if the differences in processing styles between genders would have added another layer of difficulty to the experience. When my friend, who was at the festival, slipped into a deep depression, her husband desperately wanted to support her. No matter how hard he tried, he couldn't do the one thing that those at the shooting could—he couldn't relive the event. He didn't *really* know what it was like.

For organizations, this highlights the importance of providing diverse support options that accommodate different processing styles. Some employees will benefit from group discussions and social support networks. Others will prefer individual counseling or action-oriented interventions.

Regardless of your gender, healing from trauma is possible. It's just a matter of finding the right kind of treatment and providers. Ensuring that your therapist or mental health professional understands gender differences can be a key component to healing.

For example, men may benefit from therapies that focus on processing emotions while working to challenge traditional masculine concepts that discourage emotional expression. Women might be more likely to benefit from types of therapy that incorporate social support.

For leaders, understanding these differences enables more effective crisis response and long-term support strategies. Organizations that provide both immediate action-oriented interventions and longer-term community-building support create environments where all employees can recover and thrive regardless of their natural stress response patterns.

The key is recognizing that different doesn't mean deficient. Both tend-and-befriend and fight-or-flight responses have strategic value in organizational settings. Leaders who can harness both approaches—immediate decisive action when needed and thoughtful community-building for long-term resilience—create the most robust and adaptable teams.

∾

Key Takeaways

Recognize biological differences in stress responses: Women tend toward tend-and-befriend behaviors while men lean toward fight-or-flight responses—both have strategic value in crisis management and organizational resilience.

Create diverse communication channels: Offer both verbal processing opportunities and action-oriented solutions to accommodate different coping styles and maximize team effectiveness during challenging periods.

Address gender-based workplace expectations: Challenge cultural norms that limit emotional expression for men and decision-making authority for women to unlock the full potential of diverse teams.

Develop process-driven leadership: Systematic approaches to problem-solving reduce stress and prevent impulsive decisions that disproportionately affect vulnerable employees and organizational stability.

Implement inclusive support systems: Ensure trauma recovery resources accommodate both social connection needs and individual processing preferences to support all employees effectively.

Leverage complementary leadership styles: Combine transformational and transactional approaches to create comprehensive management strategies that draw on diverse leadership strengths.

Build gender-aware mental health resources: Provide therapists and programs that understand how gender socialization affects trauma processing and recovery to maximize treatment effectiveness.

Plan strategically for stress reduction: Use systematic planning processes that engage diverse perspectives and prevent reactive leadership decisions that can destabilize teams and operations.

9

BUILDING RESILIENT COMMUNITIES

W*ell, at least you didn't die.*
The words hit me like a slap every time I heard them, which was often—more often than I ever could have imagined when I first began sharing what happened that night in Las Vegas. The phrase would emerge from well-meaning friends, concerned colleagues, distant relatives who had heard about my experience through family networks, even strangers who learned I'd survived the Route 91 shooting.

They said it with relief in their voices, with genuine gratitude that I was standing before them whole and breathing. They were trying to make me feel better, to help me focus on the positive outcome of an incomprehensibly negative experience. They wanted me to look on the bright side, to count my blessings, to feel lucky rather than traumatized.

It's true—I didn't die. That fact was undeniable, the foundation upon which everything else in my life now rested. But seeing the bright side was infinitely more complicated than anyone saying those words seemed to understand. Yes, I had survived the largest mass shooting in US history, but I had also witnessed it. I had seen a man shot and killed right beside me—one second full of life, laughing at something his friend had said, the next crumpled and still, his blood mingling with the dirt and beer-soaked ground of the venue.

My body and clothing were splattered with the blood of those who didn't survive. I had run through chaos where human beings became obstacles to climb over, where the woman who had been dancing beside me moments earlier was now motionless on the ground, where security guards stood frozen while people screamed for help that never came fast enough.

In that context, *at least you didn't die* felt coarse, almost insulting. It reduced the magnitude of what I'd experienced to a simple binary—dead or alive, lucky or unlucky, grateful or ungrateful. It suggested that survival was the only thing that mattered, that trauma was an indulgence for people who should simply appreciate being breathing.

I *was* grateful to be alive. Profoundly, viscerally grateful in ways I'd never understood before that night.

But I didn't need anyone to remind me of that gratitude, to police my emotional response to surviving something most people couldn't even imagine. What I needed was space to feel the full complexity of what survival meant—the guilt of living when others didn't, the confusion of witnessing evil that seemed to have no purpose, the exhaustion of carrying images and sounds that replayed endlessly in quiet moments.

What I needed was more than a one-line sentence encouraging me to dismiss my difficult emotions and *just be grateful*. I needed people who could sit with the messiness of trauma, who understood that surviving something terrible creates its own set of challenges that can't be resolved with positive thinking or perspective adjustments.

But I began to understand that when confronted with another person's traumatic experience, most people genuinely don't know what to say. The magnitude of what someone has survived creates a kind of conversational paralysis—how do you respond to stories that involve life and death, violence and terror, experiences so far outside normal human experience that there's no social script for processing them?

When people said hurtful things—and they did, regularly—it was likely because they were trying to relieve their own feelings of discomfort rather than genuinely help me process mine. My trauma made them uncomfortable, reminded them of their own vulnerability, forced them to confront the reality that terrible things happen to good people for no reason at all. So they deflected, trying to change the subject or lighten the mood, attempting to transform my complex experience into something simpler and more manageable.

At least you didn't die was their way of saying, *Let's focus on the good news so I don't have to think about how bad the bad news really was.* It was emotional shorthand designed to end conversations they didn't know how to have rather than support someone through experiences they didn't know how to understand.

But here's what those well-meaning people missed: Their discomfort with my trauma was creating secondary trauma. Every time someone minimized my experience, suggested I should be grateful instead of struggling or implied that survival was the only thing that mattered, they were adding layers of isolation and misunderstanding to an already experience.

I began to realize that trauma recovery isn't just an individual process—it's a community process. The way people around trauma survivors respond to their experiences can either accelerate healing or compound damage. Communities can become sources of strength and connection, or they can become additional sources of stress and alienation.

This realization had profound implications that extended far beyond my personal healing journey. As I returned to work and began rebuilding my professional life, I started noticing how organizations responded to employees experiencing various forms of trauma. I watched as well-meaning managers said similarly dismissive things to colleagues facing divorce, death of family members, health crises or other life-altering experiences.

At least it's not cancer.

At least you still have your job.

At least your kids are healthy.

The same pattern played out in conference rooms and break rooms—people trying to help by minimizing, trying to support by redirecting to gratitude, trying to show care by essentially telling trauma survivors that their experiences weren't that bad and they should focus on being lucky instead.

For leaders reading this, understanding how communities respond to trauma—both helpfully and harmfully—isn't just a matter of personal sensitivity or human resources compliance. It's crucial strategic intelligence for building organizational resilience. The way you guide your team's response to crisis, trauma and difficulty can either accelerate healing and strengthen bonds or compound trauma and fragment your organization under pressure.

Most leaders don't realize that their organizations are communities—social ecosystems where people's responses to each other's struggles determine whether individuals thrive or merely survive during difficult periods. When a crisis hits one employee, it creates ripple effects throughout the entire team. How colleagues respond to that crisis, how managers support both the affected individual and the surrounding team and how organizational culture either welcomes or dismisses difficult emotions determine whether the community becomes stronger or weaker.

The most resilient organizations aren't those where trauma never occurs—it's impossible to prevent life from happening to your employees. The most resilient organizations are those that have built community responses to trauma that actually help rather than harm, that provide genuine support rather than performative comfort, that understand the difference between toxic positivity and authentic encouragement.

In the pages that follow, you'll discover how to create communities that heal rather than harm when trauma occurs. You'll learn to recognize the difference between helpful and harmful responses to employee crises, understand how to train teams in trauma-informed communication and build organizational cultures where people feel safe bringing their full experiences to work without fear of judgment or minimization.

You'll explore practical strategies for mobilizing community support during crisis, creating lasting symbols of connection that help trauma survivors feel less isolated and leveraging the heroic responses that often emerge during organizational challenges. Most importantly, you'll understand how communities that learn to respond effectively to individual trauma become more resilient to collective challenges, creating competitive advantages that can't be replicated by organizations that treat employee well-being as an individual responsibility rather than a community commitment.

Because here's what I learned through my own recovery and in the years I've spent building trauma-informed teams: The same communities that know how to respond helpfully to individual crisis are the ones that thrive during organizational upheaval, market disruption and collective challenges. The same communication skills that help trauma survivors feel supported are the ones that create psychological safety for innovation and risk-taking. The same community bonds that accelerate individual healing are the ones that create organizational resilience during difficult seasons.

The question isn't whether your employees will face trauma—they will, they *are*, in forms ranging from personal loss to global pandemics to industry disruption. The question is whether your organization will become a community that compounds that trauma through well-meaning but harmful responses or one that transforms individual pain into collective strength through genuine understanding and support.

The difference between these two outcomes isn't accidental. It's the result of intentional choices about how communities respond to difficulty, and it determines whether organizations emerge from crisis stronger or merely survive to face the next challenge.

Creating Trauma-Informed Communication Standards

According to the US Department of Veterans Affairs, "Sometimes friends, family and co-workers can disappear after a loss. They may not know what to say, worry they will say the wrong thing or overstep, fear causing more pain, feel somehow guilty about the death or fear they can't do enough to make the grieving person feel better."[35]

For starters, it's important for colleagues and supervisors of trauma survivors to understand that no one-line response is going to take away feelings of pain. *At least you didn't die* isn't a magical statement that can take away feelings of sorrow or PTSD.

It would have been much better if someone had offered me support by first listening and then validating what I'd gone through. Something like, *Wow, that must have been awful!* Or, *Thank you for sharing that with me. It must have been really hard to relive that.*

It's perfectly understandable if someone doesn't know what to say. In fact, they can even use that as a response. *Wow. I don't even know what to say* is a better response than offering something you're not sure the survivor is ready to hear.

There were other responses that were not so obviously well-intentioned. Some, rather than listening and validating, tried to engage me in discussions of conspiracy theories. People thought that, since I was there, I must have insider information. This bothered me because I was focused on healing my trauma by using coping skills like running to clear my mind when I couldn't stop ruminating.

If someone has questions about the details of a tragic event, it's important for them to check in with themselves. *What is the purpose of asking this question? Is it helpful to the survivor? Was I just trying to satisfy my morbid curiosity?*

According to The Grief Recovery Center, certain phrases consistently harm trauma survivors, while others provide genuine support.[36] Understanding why specific language helps or hurts reveals the deeper dynamics of trauma-informed communication that every leader needs to master.

Phrases That May Risk Causing Additional Harm:

"**It's time to move on**" fundamentally misunderstands how trauma affects the brain and nervous system. This phrase implies that healing operates on external time-lines rather than internal processing needs. When someone says this to a trauma survivor, they're essentially demanding that the person override their biological recovery process to accommodate others' discomfort with their pain. For trauma survivors, this message reinforces shame about their healing pace and suggests that their struggle is inconveniencing others. In workplace settings, this attitude creates environments where employees hide their difficulties rather than seek support, leading to decreased performance and increased turnover.

"**It couldn't have been that bad**" directly invalidates the survivor's experience and perception of reality. Trauma survivors often struggle with self-doubt about their memories and reactions—this phrase amplifies that uncertainty and suggests their pain is exaggerated or manufactured. When leaders or colleagues dismiss employee experiences this way, they communicate that the organization doesn't trust employees' judgment about their own lives. This destroys psychological safety and prevents honest communication about workplace challenges, creating cultures where problems fester rather than get addressed.

"Stop being so negative" treats trauma symptoms as character flaws rather than biological responses to overwhelming experiences. This phrase suggests that trauma survivors are choosing their emotional state and could simply decide to feel better if they tried harder. It ignores the neurological reality that trauma creates lasting changes in brain function that require time and often professional intervention to resolve. In organizations, this attitude leads to managers viewing struggling employees as attitude problems rather than people needing support, resulting in disciplinary actions that compound trauma rather than address its underlying causes.

"It could always be worse" forces trauma survivors into comparative suffering, as if pain operates on a hierarchy where only the most extreme experiences deserve acknowledgment. This phrase dismisses legitimate struggles by suggesting that unless someone has endured the absolute worst possible scenario, their pain isn't worth attention or support. When workplace leaders use this logic, they create environments where employees must compete for recognition of their difficulties, leading to cultures where people either hide their struggles or exaggerate them to receive basic compassion.

Responses That Can Provide Genuine Support:

"**I'll be here for you, no matter what**" offers unconditional presence without placing demands on the survivor's healing process. This phrase communicates reliability and removes the pressure trauma survivors often feel to "get better" quickly to maintain relationships. It acknowledges that recovery takes time and may involve setbacks, while assuring the person that support won't disappear during difficult moments. In workplace contexts, this approach creates psychological safety where employees can focus on both healing and performance without fear that temporary struggles will jeopardize their position or relationships.

"**I will support you in every way I know how**" acknowledges both genuine care and human limitations. This phrase offers concrete help while being honest about the supporter's capacity, which prevents overpromising and builds trust through realistic expectations. It invites collaboration in determining what support looks like rather than imposing assumptions about what the trauma survivor needs. For leaders, this approach models vulnerability and authenticity while demonstrating commitment to employee well-being within appropriate professional boundaries.

"**None of this was your fault**" directly addresses the shame and self-blame that often accompany traumatic experiences. Trauma survivors frequently torture themselves with "what if" scenarios, wondering if they could have prevented or responded differently to their experiences. This phrase interrupts those shame cycles and reinforces that trauma happens to people, not because of their failures or weaknesses. When organizational leaders communicate this message, they prevent trauma survivors from taking inappropriate responsibility for external events and help them focus energy on healing rather than self-recrimination.

"Do you want to talk about it?" offers opportunity for processing without creating an obligation to share. This phrase respects the trauma survivor's autonomy over their own story while creating space for connection if desired. It acknowledges that talking can be helpful for many people while recognizing that forced sharing often causes additional harm. In workplace settings, this approach helps managers gauge employee needs without pressuring disclosure, allowing for appropriate support that doesn't violate privacy or professional boundaries.

The fundamental difference between harmful and helpful responses lies in their approach to control. Harmful phrases attempt to control the trauma survivor's experience, timeline or emotional expression to reduce the supporter's discomfort. Helpful phrases acknowledge the trauma survivor's expertise about their own experience while offering genuine support that doesn't impose conditions or timelines on recovery. For organizations, this distinction reveals why traditional approaches to employee assistance often fail. Programs that focus on quickly returning employees to "normal" function rather than supporting authentic healing create additional stress for trauma survivors while failing to address the root causes of performance issues. Companies that understand trauma-informed communication principles create environments where employees can access support without fear of judgment, leading to faster recovery and stronger long-term performance.

For organizations, establishing clear communication guidelines prevents well-meaning colleagues from inadvertently causing additional harm. When leaders train their teams in trauma-informed language, they create environments where employees feel safe seeking support rather than hiding their struggles.

Sometimes, there is no need for words at all. After the shooting, so many people that I love showed up for me without words. Instead, friends sent flowers and chocolates. This showed me that they cared and made me feel loved and supported.

When in Doubt, *Be the Good*

One of the most memorable things that someone did for me was a gesture that perfectly captured how meaningful support can be layered with both comfort and purpose. My friend Erin, who had been watching me struggle with the aftermath of the shooting for weeks, gave me a beautiful handmade wooden sign that would become one of my most treasured possessions.

At first glance, the sign appeared to carry a simple, if powerful, message: *Believe There Is Good in the World*, the kind of inspirational phrase you might find in a home decor store. But as I examined it more closely and turned it over in my mind, Sarah pointed out something remarkable—certain letters were highlighted in a different color, creating a hidden message within the obvious one.

BElieve

THEre

Is

GOOD

In

The

world

When you read only the highlighted letters, they spell out **be the good**.

The dual message hit me with unexpected force. On the surface, the sign offered comfort and hope during a time when I was struggling to see either in the world around me. After witnessing such senseless violence, after seeing the worst of humanity played out in real time, I desperately needed reminders that goodness still existed somewhere in the universe.

But the hidden message went deeper, transforming passive hope into active purpose. It wasn't just telling me to believe good existed—it was challenging me to become part of that good. It acknowledged my pain while simultaneously suggesting that my experience, terrible as it was, could be transformed into something that contributed positively to the world.

This wasn't the kind of toxic positivity that so many people had offered with their "at least you didn't die" comments. Sarah wasn't asking me to pretend the trauma hadn't happened or to suppress my difficult emotions in favor of artificial gratitude. Instead, she was offering a framework for meaning-making that honored both my suffering and my potential for growth.

The sign represented everything that effective trauma support should be: It acknowledged the darkness I'd experienced while pointing toward light, provided comfort while inspiring action and offered hope that was grounded in purpose rather than empty optimism. It didn't minimize my pain or rush my healing—it simply suggested that when I was ready, my experience could become a source of strength for others.

Years later, that message has become central to how I approach both leadership and life. The trauma I experienced at Route 91 didn't disappear or get resolved through positive thinking, but it has been transformed into purpose. The pain became fuel for helping other trauma survivors, the experience became wisdom I could share with colleagues facing their own difficult seasons and the darkness became a backdrop that makes light more visible and precious.

For leaders, the message behind Sarah's sign illustrates the power of meaningful support that provides both comfort and direction. When employees face trauma, crisis or significant life challenges, the most effective organizational responses don't just offer sympathy—they help people find ways to transform their experiences into strength that benefits both individual recovery and collective resilience.

This approach requires moving beyond simple employee assistance programs that focus solely on returning people to previous levels of functioning. Instead, trauma-informed organizations create opportunities for employees to find meaning and purpose in their struggles, to contribute to solutions that help others facing similar challenges and to discover how their personal growth can enhance their professional contributions.

Authentic community support can look starkly different from corporate-mandated wellness initiatives.

Sarah's gift was personal, thoughtful and tailored specifically to what she knew I needed during that particular phase of my recovery. She hadn't read a manual about trauma support or followed a company protocol—she had paid attention to my specific situation and created something unique that addressed both my immediate need for hope and my deeper need for purpose.

This level of authentic support can't be manufactured through policies or procedures, but it can be cultivated through organizational cultures that encourage genuine care between colleagues, that provide space for people to bring their whole selves to work and that recognize the strategic value of employees who transform personal adversity into professional wisdom.

When organizations create environments where people feel safe sharing their struggles and colleagues feel empowered to respond with creativity and genuine care, they build the kind of community resilience that becomes a competitive advantage during challenging times. The same qualities that enabled Sarah to create meaningful support for my trauma recovery are the ones that help teams navigate organizational crises with grace, innovation and mutual support.

The Strategic Value of Swift Community Response

Community plays a vital role in helping people heal from trauma, and organizations are uniquely positioned to mobilize this support quickly and effectively. From the very first moment that the shooting started, a community was forming around me. My husband took on the role as a leader and helped me and others run to safety. When we made it to safety, I was met with a community of strangers hugging and offering support.

Many people attending the Route 91 festival were first responders. Off-duty police officers, EMT drivers, firefighters, paramedics and people in the military were all in attendance. When the shooting started, they didn't just run for their lives. Instead, they jumped into action. They used their knowledge and expertise to actively help people get to safety.

Regular people, without any training at all, also offered the help they could. When someone fell, they picked them up and threw them over their shoulders. When someone couldn't get an ambulance, they put them in their own cars and sped away to the hospital. When someone needed lifesaving medical attention, they provided it using what skills they had.

Many civilians, military and police were given honorable awards for their heroism during the event. To name a few: Martin Heffernan, assistant Scoutmaster, was honored by Boy Scouts of America with the

Honor Award with Crossed Palms. Brittany Speer, an EMT from UCLA, received a Medal of Courage from the University of California Police Department for her bravery in setting up a triage area and treating victims while the shooter was still active. Sgt. Austin Cox and Sgt. Michael Vura, helicopter mechanics with the US Marines, received the Navy and Marine Corps Medal for braving gunfire to save victims.[37]

According to *Psychology Today*, heroes nourish our connections with other people and build stronger communities. "If the hero is an effective one, he or she performs actions that exemplify and affirm the community's most cherished values. The validation of a shared worldview (told vividly in storytelling) cements social bonds."[38]

For leaders, this demonstrates the importance of recognizing and celebrating employees who step up during a crisis. When organizations highlight heroic responses rather than focusing solely on problems, they reinforce values and inspire others to act courageously when faced with challenges.

According to Fox News, "Las Vegas shooting survivors have embraced 'Country Strong' as a mantra for their tight-knit, supportive community that has emerged in the wake of the country's deadliest mass shooting. What were once strangers at the Route 91 Harvest country music festival have become family. They meet up at other concerts with matching shirts and ribbons and have monthly support groups and raise money for those struggling."[39]

We became a community of survivors that shared an unbreakable bond forged in the face of tragedy. Whether it was through text threads, memorial gatherings or sharing stories online, we found healing in our connection. What once was a group of individuals united by music became a resilient, compassionate community that continues to honor the lives lost.

Creating Lasting Symbols of Connection

Following the shooting, survivors responded with an outpouring of compassion that created lasting support. One survivor made Route 91 survivor bumper stickers— an orange ribbon with the date of the festival. I got one for my car, initially just thinking it was a way to show support.

But over the years, there have been countless times that someone saw my bumper sticker and stopped me. They shared that either they themselves were there that night or a loved one was there. Once, a stranger stopped me in a parking lot. "I saw your bumper sticker," she said. "I had a friend who was there that night. She's not the same person. I'm so sorry that happened to you."

In those moments, I felt less alone. What happened to me was part of something that so many people experienced. There were over 20,000 people at the concert that night. We scattered back to our homes across the country, carrying with us the memories and pain. I was forever connected to something bigger—a group of people that turned into a community of survivors.

Another example of healing through community is the Las Vegas Community Healing Garden. This memorial garden features a wall of remembrance, a grove of trees, shrubs, flowers, walkways and benches. The construction of the park was built by hundreds of volunteers—some Route 91 concertgoers, but many citizens from Las Vegas who were heartbroken by the news and wanted to give back to their beloved community.

For organizations, creating symbols of shared experience—whether physical mementos, digital spaces or recurring traditions—helps trauma survivors feel connected and less isolated. These symbols become anchors that remind employees they're part of something larger than their individual struggle.

Building Organizational Community That Heals

It's not just community leaders who offer healing. Leaders of workplaces and organizations can build strong communities that create resilience before a crisis hits. When the culture of the workplace has a sense of community with strong bonds and tight teams, it makes a difference on a larger scale. Employees are at the center of any organization's success, so creating a company culture where employees feel safe and validated is essential for the company to thrive.

I love to build strong teams and create a sense of community in the workplace. The steps I take are to:

- Establish trust through transparency. When I am transparent, it gives permission for employees to be their true selves.
- Follow through with commitments and admit to my mistakes. If I say I'm going to do something, I do it. If I make a mistake, I am the first to apologize and let them know I'm the one responsible.
- Allow for open communication. I always tell my team the truth. I'm clear and direct, and I try not to surprise them with unexpected tasks or issues. I make my office a safe place for them to come and talk to me when issues arise.
- Set clear roles and expectations. I make it clear what I expect of employees by offering things like clear deadlines so we can all succeed together. Being clear is being kind and respectful. When employees know what is expected, they can better prepare, plan and execute.
- Celebrate wins on a regular basis. I ask my team to set monthly personal development

goals, then present their goals and how they were successful. As a team, we review and provide feedback and applause. All team members contribute to each other's success. Investing in my team's personal development shows that I care about them as humans, not just employees.

- Have fun together. I bring excitement by organizing activities that are completely unrelated to work—happy hour meetups, fitness challenges and even March Madness bracket competitions. These experiences foster healthy competition and bring laughs and joy among us. A team that is having fun together will grow stronger bonds that will serve the organization during difficult times.

I believe that building strong bonds among employees means seeing them as more than just people who work for me. One way I do this is by facilitating connections among team members on topics that interest them beyond work. For example, we have a group thread specific to parents. The parents on the team can share pictures of their kids or ask for help on specific parenting topics. This helps employees feel connected to one another on a level deeper than work. We can support each other in the office, but also in our lives outside of work.

For leaders, these community-building practices aren't just feel-good initiatives—they're strategic investments in organizational resilience. When a crisis hits, teams with strong emotional bonds recover faster and emerge stronger than groups that are merely functional colleagues.

The Strategic Value of Team Retreats

I'm a big believer in team building through off-site team retreats. According to *Justworks*, off-site retreats have multiple employee benefits. "Being in a new space that is solely dedicated to a certain project or task will help your company gain more focus. Employees feel dedicated to the cause. And more focus leads to productivity."[40]

The article continues: "Whether your staff retreat is a picnic at the zoo or a scavenger hunt inside your city's most famous museum, it'll help bond people together. Being somewhere new and dedicating yourself to a mission makes team members come out of the off-site feeling stronger together."

I like to start retreats with an icebreaker. I ask each member to share a fun fact about themselves or something interesting that no one on the team knows. This allows us to get a glimpse of each other's personal interests and lives. At our retreats, we also take time to connect with one another. I find that when we are spending time together without the additional stress of work tasks, we become more creative and open.

I love to foster team-building exercises during our off-site retreats. One time we took uncooked spaghetti and marshmallows. The challenge was to use only those materials to see which team could build the tallest tower. As a leader, I loved watching the teams get creative! They developed remarkable methods for making their towers taller than their competitors. It gave me insight into their personalities and styles while giving my team members lots of laughs.

At our retreats, we engage in a "get-to-know-you hour," in which I ask each team member to find another person they don't know very well and spend time together on a walk or just hanging out.

When leaders develop strong teams through experiences like retreats, they create organizational resilience that extends beyond the workplace. Strong teams become advocates for each other during personal crises and champions for the organization during professional challenges.

Examples of Community Resilience in Action

In the wake of the attack, the Legal Aid Center of Southern Nevada posted an article called "91 Points of Light: In Las Vegas' Darkest Hour, Humanity Shone Brightly."[41] It listed 91 stories of heroism, healing, helping and hope that occurred. Below are just some of the ways that individuals, communities and organizations showed up:

- *In the hours after the attack, lines of people snaked around local donation centers as people waited hours to give blood.*
- *Zappos raised $2.7 million for Route 91 survivors and helped pay funeral expenses for a number of those killed in the shooting.*
- *J.H. Williams III and Wendy Wright-Williams created "Where We Live," a 300-page anthology comic book about the shooting that raised more than $100000 for the victims and their families.*
- *Downtown Las Vegas music entrepreneur Ronald Corso invited select artists into his studio to record covers of country songs for a compilation record benefiting Route 91 survivors.*

The list of remarkable acts of kindness goes on. Yet in the aftermath of tragedy, these powerful stories are often overshadowed. Instead of highlighting the humanity that rises from heartbreak, the spotlight too often shifts to lawsuits, conspiracy theories and everything that went wrong.

Since that tragic night, I've chosen to heal by focusing on the goodness that still exists in the world. I look around and see love and support surrounding me

—my devoted husband who saved my life, our two beautiful children, my incredible mom and my dad, who may no longer be here in body but whose presence I feel with me every single day.

I draw strength from my friends, my colleagues, those I have the honor to lead and my unbreakable Route 91 family. Every day, I witness acts of kindness, compassion and resilience. I see good people doing good things—and I am grateful to be a part of a community where light continues to shine so brightly, even in the face of darkness.

For leaders, this choice of focus becomes a strategic decision. Organizations that emphasize stories of courage, compassion and resilience rather than dwelling on problems create cultures where people feel empowered to act heroically when faced with challenges. When you consistently highlight the good in your community, you inspire more good to emerge.

The way organizations respond to crises—whether focusing on heroism or harm, connection or blame, solutions or problems—determines whether they emerge from trauma stronger or weaker. Leaders who understand this principle can transform even the most devastating experiences into sources of organizational strength and community resilience.

∼

KEY TAKEAWAYS

Train employees in trauma-informed communication: Provide specific language guidelines for responding to colleagues experiencing crisis or grief to prevent well-meaning but harmful responses.

Create multiple support channels: Establish both formal and informal support systems, including peer groups, professional resources and online communities to accommodate different processing styles.

Design meaningful connection rituals: Implement regular practices that build emotional bonds beyond work tasks to create resilience before crisis hits.

Invest in team retreat experiences: Use off-site gatherings to deepen relationships and create shared positive memories that strengthen organizational resilience during challenging times.

Establish clear crisis response protocols: Develop systematic approaches for mobilizing community support when trauma affects your organization to prevent chaos and ensure consistent care.

Leverage storytelling for healing: Create safe spaces for employees to share experiences and build understanding across different trauma responses to foster empathy and connection.

Build symbols of solidarity: Develop visual representations of shared experience that help trauma survivors feel connected and less isolated in their recovery journey.

Connect workplace community to broader impact: Encourage collective volunteer efforts and community engagement that extend organizational bonds beyond the office and create meaning.

Focus on heroism over harm: When discussing traumatic events, emphasize stories of courage, compassion and resilience rather than dwelling on perpetrators or conspiracies to inspire positive action.

10

IMPLEMENTING TRAUMA-INFORMED LEADERSHIP

With time, I felt as if I was outgrowing my role at Walmart. I'd been working there for a long time and was close to earning my retention bonus. I was ready to move on, but it didn't seem right to leave just yet.

Then, Walmart made an announcement that changed everything. It established a new home office in Bentonville, Arkansas and stated that to foster a more unified work culture, executives would need to relocate and operate from the Bentonville offices. Walmart was asking that I either relocate or leave the company without my bonus. It felt unfair.

I live in the house I grew up in. It's my place of refuge and safety. I have built a community around me filled with people I love. My two small children are now becoming involved in school and community activities in the same places I did when I was a child. To say that my roots run deep in Orange County is an understatement.

Over the years, I've made a name for myself in the industry. I'm considered a leader and an influencer. My track record for leading successful teams speaks for itself, and because of that, executives from competitor companies have always tried to recruit me. Even though I'd turned them all down in the past, it was now time to consider what other opportunities were out there.

For leaders facing similar organizational changes, this scenario illustrates a critical principle: When companies force employees to choose between their established support systems and their careers, they often lose their most valuable talent. Trauma-informed leaders understand that community connections aren't luxuries—they're essential foundations for employee resilience and performance.

Strategic Career Transitions in a Trauma-Informed Context

Wendy Greenland, the CEO of Openforce, was someone I'd known for years. When Walmart acquired DDI, Wendy approached me about coming to work for her. At the time, it wasn't the right move, but I was always interested in the work she was doing. I'd never worked for a female CEO before—I'd watched Wendy from afar as she successfully grew her team and business.

When I got the news from Walmart that I was being asked to relocate, I reached out to some of the CEOs who had tried to recruit me. I called Wendy and let her know that I was considering leaving Walmart. To my surprise, she was still very interested in hiring me. We hopped on a few phone calls to discuss the possibilities of me working at Openforce. Quickly, I realized how much I loved the mission of the company. Openforce is a contract management platform that helps independent contractors successfully run their businesses. Because of Openforce, small businesses have successfully grown into large companies.

Wendy knew how passionate I was about the success of small businesses in the industry. I love nothing more than to see people succeed, and Openforce has a vital role in making that happen. Plus, I would now work with a female CEO, which was a rare opportunity in this space.

Within a week, I was signing a contract to become the new senior vice president of enterprise Sales. Wendy helped Openforce meet my needs. She even agreed to pay me a bonus to make up for the retention bonus I lost by leaving Walmart.

This transition exemplifies how trauma-informed leaders approach talent acquisition and retention. Rather than forcing employees into rigid corporate structures, they recognize that supporting individual needs often yields better business outcomes. Organizations that accommodate employees' community connections and family situations are more likely to attract and retain top talent, especially those who have developed resilience through overcoming significant challenges.

My biggest concern was that, by changing roles, I might have to step down from ECA, the board position that I'd grown to love. Luckily, though, Wendy saw my position on the board as a strong asset in my new role. The work I was doing on the board brought opportunity and exposure to Openforce, so it was an obvious choice for me to maintain my role.

Prior to the Route 91 festival shooting, I had no idea what I wanted to do with my career. I hadn't yet figured out my passion or my purpose. While experiencing the shooting was one of the worst things that happened to me, my second chance at life kick-started my post-traumatic growth. When faced with death, you begin to see life differently.

I've worked hard to create a life for myself that adds value not just for me and my family, but also the world. Not only do I provide high-level executives a roadmap for understanding trauma, security and safety solutions, but I'm highly regarded in the transportation industry.

In my early days at DDI, my boss, Aaron, told me,

"Carly, once you gain confidence, you will be unstoppable!" After coming face-to-face with death, I knew I could no longer afford to doubt myself. I began to embrace my strengths fully—and let them speak louder than my fears and flaws. Aaron was right! My career has exploded since I've developed confidence.

Practical Implementation of Safety-Conscious Leadership

Part of my job requires me to spend time in crowds. I'm expected to attend conferences, summits and other large-scale business events on a regular basis. My outlook on these events has certainly changed.

Safety is obviously a top priority—but so are connection and support. If you see me at one of these events, you can count on me to know where the nearest exit is—but you can also ask me to listen if something's weighing on your mind or if you're carrying a worry you need to share.

After everything I've been through, I feel it's my duty to offer support. I'm never too busy or too important to notice when someone is hurting or needs a friend. I'm grateful that my experience with trauma helped remind me of these values. Because of this, I've become a better leader and advocate for my employees.

This approach to leadership—combining heightened awareness of physical safety with emotional availability—creates a model that other leaders can adopt. Organizations benefit when leaders model both vigilance and vulnerability, demonstrating that strength includes acknowledging and addressing potential threats while remaining open to supporting others through their struggles.

Since the shooting, I've continued to enjoy all sorts of live music. I've seen Thomas Rhett, Zac Brown, Kenny Chesney and Morgan Wallen concerts. I also attend our local lake concerts every other week during the summer months.

It's not always easy to put myself back in these sorts of situations. I may always have a heightened sense of awareness, and I never go into a crowd without an exit strategy. But since that awful night, I've endeavored not to let the actions of one troubled individual take away the things I cherish most. With each show I attend, I develop a greater appreciation for my life. I know how lucky I am to be alive and able to continue to do the things I love.

For leaders, this demonstrates the importance of modeling resilience while maintaining appropriate caution. When employees see leaders continuing to engage fully in life while taking reasonable precautions, they learn that trauma doesn't have to define or limit them—it can inform and strengthen them.

Leading with Empathy and Strategic Intelligence

These days, I have a deeper understanding of the emotional experiences people go through. If someone I work with is irritated or angry, I understand they might be facing more than just a hard day at work. Maybe they feel stressed because of relationship issues or a sick parent. Maybe they're tired from a night of caring for their baby. Maybe they are dealing with trauma and grief.

For me, leading isn't just about hitting targets and reaching goals. Those things are important to keep a business running. But there's something deeper that occurs when you choose to lead with empathy, kindness and support. You foster an environment of connection.

Everyone wants to feel like they're part of something bigger. They want to feel connected to a mission or a purpose. No matter if the person I'm working with is a driver or a CEO, I can have a positive influence just by connecting. I see them as humans first.

Something as simple as genuinely saying, "How are you doing?" or "You can come talk to me" can go a long way in improving a person's overall well-being.

This human-first approach to leadership creates measurable business outcomes. When employees feel seen and supported, they demonstrate higher engagement, increased productivity and greater loyalty to the organization. The investment in emotional intelligence and empathetic leadership practices pays dividends in retention, performance and company culture.

Building High-Performance Teams Through Connection

Recently, I attended an incredible couple of days at Openforce HQ with our leadership team. As a team, we dug into challenges, mapped out improvements and most importantly, grew together by connecting and getting to know one another. Listening to the people in the room and learning from their experiences was a reminder of the strength that comes from trust, accountability and resilience.

Every moment I was there reminded me how lucky I am to be part of such a strong, driven and supportive team. When teams spend intentional time working together to develop solutions, they come out more aligned, more connected and more motivated than ever.

This type of intensive team development represents a strategic investment in organizational resilience. By creating structured opportunities for deep connection and collaborative problem-solving, leaders build teams that can weather any crisis. The time spent on relationship-building and trust development is not separate from business objectives—it's fundamental to achieving them.

Recently, I was asked to be a return guest on the

Last2First Podcast. Getting to speak on podcasts is something I thought I'd never want to do. Now, I can't wait for my next invite. I love sharing about what I've learned to help others become better leaders.

In this episode, I represented Openforce and shared the microphone with my CEO, Wendy. We discussed our shared beliefs in helping people succeed, challenges in the business and ways to improve strategies in the industry. Toward the end of our interview, the host, Jason Burns, wanted to discuss the shooting. "How has that experience shaped you personally and professionally?" he asked.

I teared up. I never know when the emotions of that night are going to hit me. This was one of those times. I took a deep breath and explained, "Yeah, I have trauma. But everyone has a certain level of hardships that they are going through," I said through tears.

"I have more empathy than I had before," I said and explained how I help my mentees, employees or co-workers realize that they can get through hard things.

This moment of vulnerability during a professional interview demonstrates a crucial principle of trauma-informed leadership: Authenticity creates connection and trust. When leaders model emotional honesty—showing that strength includes acknowledging struggles—they give their teams permission to be human while maintaining professional excellence.

Organizations that encourage this type of authentic

leadership see improved psychological safety, increased innovation and stronger team cohesion. Employees feel safe to take risks, admit mistakes and bring their full selves to work when they see leaders doing the same.

A Framework for Organizational Implementation

Being a survivor of trauma isn't something that anyone would ask for. But within a crisis, organizations can find an opportunity. The frameworks I've developed for understanding and supporting traumatized employees, building safety-conscious cultures and creating resilient teams can transform how businesses operate.

If there's one message from this book, it's that trauma isn't reserved for those who have experienced mass violence. It's all around us. Accidents, loss, illness and upheaval are unfortunately part of the human experience. As a leader, it's crucial to understand that employees will experience pain and grief at some point. This book provides a roadmap to help leaders navigate these intense situations in a caring and supportive way that benefits both individuals and organizations.

Organizations that implement trauma-informed leadership practices see measurable improvements in:

Employee retention and engagement: Teams feel supported through difficult times rather than abandoned, creating fierce loyalty and commitment.

Innovation and risk-taking: Psychological safety

enables creative problem-solving and strategic thinking that drives competitive advantage.

Crisis response capabilities: Organizations with trauma-informed cultures recover faster from disruptions and emerge stronger from challenges.

Leadership pipeline strength: Employees who receive support through challenges often become the most resilient and effective leaders.

Customer relationships: Empathetic, authentic leadership creates stronger external partnerships and client loyalty.

Financial performance: All of the above factors contribute to improved bottom-line results and sustainable growth.

Your Next Steps as a Trauma-Informed Leader

The journey toward trauma-informed leadership begins with a single decision: to see your employees as complete human beings who bring both tremendous capability and inevitable vulnerability to work. From that foundation, you can build systems, policies and practices that honor both business objectives and human dignity.

Start small. Choose one framework from this book—perhaps the return-to-work protocols from Chapter Two or the vulnerability practices from Chapter Six—and implement it thoughtfully within your team. Measure the results not just in traditional business metrics, but in employee feedback, team cohesion and your own experience as a leader.

As you build competence and confidence, expand your approach. Train your management team. Update your policies. Create support systems. Build the kind of organization where people don't just survive their worst days—they thrive beyond them.

The world needs leaders who understand that supporting human beings through trauma isn't just morally right—it's strategically smart. When you invest in trauma-informed leadership, you're not just helping individuals heal. You're building the kind of resilient, adaptive, high-performing organization that can succeed in any environment.

Your employees are watching to see how you'll respond when a crisis hits their lives. Will you be the leader who helps them find their way back to strength?

The choice—the opportunity—is yours.

~

Key Takeaways

Implement gradually with measurable outcomes: Start with one trauma-informed practice and track both employee feedback and business metrics before expanding to create sustainable change.

Recognize organizational change as potential trauma: Major shifts like relocations, acquisitions or restructuring can trigger trauma responses that require thoughtful management and support.

Create flexible career pathways: Support employees' community connections and family needs rather than forcing choices between personal stability and professional growth.

Model authentic vulnerability: Leaders who show appropriate emotional honesty create psychological safety that enables higher performance and innovation.

Invest in relationship-building as business strategy: Time spent on team connection and trust development directly impacts organizational resilience and adaptability.

Develop trauma-informed recruitment practices: Attract and retain top talent by demonstrating genuine care for employee well-being and work-life integration.

Measure success holistically: Track employee engagement, retention, innovation metrics and customer satisfaction alongside traditional financial performance indicators.

Build sustainability into trauma-informed practices: Create systems and policies that maintain a supportive culture even during leadership transitions or organizational changes.

AFTERWORD

As I reflect on my life, my journey from the trauma of the Route 91 shooting to the opportunities I've embraced since, I realize how far I've come—both personally and professionally. Without the lessons that I've learned, I wouldn't be the leader that I am today. I've discovered that trauma-informed leadership is not just about helping people recover; it's about helping people thrive. I want to create a culture that values the whole person, not just the employee.

When organizations take the time to understand and honor the personal struggles of their employees, they develop a level of performance and loyalty that's unmatched. I feel honored to be a leader at Openforce and the ECA board. I will use these opportunities to continue to build teams that are connected, supported and encouraged.

I know that I will face more life challenges. I may even face more trauma. But I will not be led by fear. These days, I view challenges as opportunities to grow, learn and strengthen my skills. Each challenge I face reminds me that I am human and furthers my commitment to being someone who leads with empathy and support.

ACKNOWLEDGEMENTS

First, I want to thank my mom and dad for always believing in me and supporting both my brother Cody and me, even when times got tough.

Second, I want to thank my first two mentors, Aaron Hageman and Adam Dodge, for always seeing the value I can bring to the table, always having my back and lifting me up both personally and professionally.

Last, and most importantly, I want to thank my family: my kids, Olivia and Logan, who are my inspiration every day, and my husband, Kevin, for always going along with my crazy ideas and supporting me no matter what. I wouldn't be able to do what I do without you. Love you!

BIBLIOGRAPHY/CITATIONS

[1] World Health Organization. "Post-Traumatic Stress Disorder." May 27, 2024. https://who.int/news-room/fact-sheets/detail/post-traumatic-stress-disorder.

[2] Bremmer, J. Douglass. "Traumatic Stress: Effects on The Brain." *National Library of Medicine*. https://pmc.ncbi.nlm.nih.gov/articles/PMC3181836/.

[3] Cherry, Karen. "What Is the Fight or Flight Response?" *Very Well Mind*, June 17, 2024. https://verywellmind.com/what-is-the-fight-or-flight-response-2795194.

[4] Taylor, Martin. "What Does Fight, Flight, Freeze, Fawn Mean?" *WebMD*, June 24, 2024. https://webmd.com/mental-health/what-does-fight-flight-freeze-fawn-mean.

[5] Effa, Cecilia. "The Brain's Response to Trauma: Understanding the Impact of PTSD." *Medical News Today*, August 14, 2024. https://medicalnewstoday.com/articles/how-does-ptsd-affect-the-brain.

[6] "Dyer, Regina. "The Myth of Replaceability: Preparing for the Loss of Key Employees." *SHRM Business*, January 21, 2025. https://www.shrm.org/executive-network/insights/myth-replaceability-preparing-loss-key-employees"

[7] Minnick, John. "How psychological safety affects employee productivity." *Ragan*, April 14, 2023. https://www.ragan.com/how-psychological-safety-affects-employee-productivity/

[8] US Department of Veterans Affairs. "How Common Is PTSD in Adults?" March 26, 2025. https://www.ptsd.va.gov/understand/common/common_adults.asp

[9] Tyrrell, Patrick; Seneca Harberger; and Waquar Siddiqui. "Kubler-Ross Stages of Dying and Subsequent Models of Grief." *NCBI*, February 26, 1993. https://ncbi.nlm.nih.gov/books/NBK507885/.

[10] US Department of Labor. "Family Medical Leave Act." https://dol.gov/general/topic/benefits-leave/fmla.

[11] World Economic Forum. "How To Navigate Grief In The Post-Pandemic Workplace." January 31, 2022. https://weforum.org/stories/2022/01/how-to-navigate-grief-in-the-post-pandemic-workplace.

[12] Sympathy Brands. "Death, Grieving, Bereavement: The Impact to Business." https://www.sympathybrands.com/leadership-insights/death-grieving-bereavement

[13] Cane, Aine. "Since 2020, There Have Been About 500 Shootings at Major Supermarket Chains in America, Study Finds." *Business Insider.* https://businessinsider.com/supermarket-shootings-america-statistics-grocery-store-guns-2022-6.

[14] US Department of Labor, Occupational Safety and Health Administration. "Recommended Practices For Safety and Health Programs." https://osha.gov/safety-management.

[15] Rochford, Tim. "Why Include Self Defense Training Into Corporate Wellness Programs." *Corporate Wellness Magazine.* https://corporatewellnessmagazine.com/article/why-include-self.

[16] Shaw, Jack. "How Safe Do Your Employees Feel in the Workplace?" *Big Ideas For Small Businesses,* June 19, 2024. https://bigideasforsmallbusiness.com/how-safe-do-your-employees-feel-in-the-workplace/.

[17] *Psychology Today.* "Post-Traumatic Growth." https://psychologytoday.com/us/basics/post-traumatic-growth.

[18] Hamilton, Diana. "5 Ways To Help Employees Find Purpose: Why It Matters More Than Perks." *Forbes,* November 10, 2024. https://forbes.com/sites/dianehamilton/2024/11/10/5-ways-to-help-employees-find-purpose-why-it-matters-more-than-perks/.

[19] Mayo Clinic. "Positive Thinking: Stop Negative Self-Talk to Reduce Stress." https://mayoclinic.org/healthy-lifestyle/stress-management/in-depth/positive-thinking/art-20043950.

[20] Romero, Luis E. "The Power Of Vulnerability In Leadership: Experts Say Authenticity And Honesty Can Move People And Achieve Results." *Forbes,* March 8, 2023. https://forbes.-

com/sites/luisromero/2023/03/08/the-power-of-vulnerability-in-leadership-experts-say-authenticity-and-honesty-can-move-people-and-achieve-results/.

[21] Boise State College of Business and Economics. "Cultivating Ethical Business Practices in Your Organization." March 2024. https://boisestate.edu/cobe/blog/2024/03/cultivating-ethical-business-practices-in-your-organization/.

[22] Glass, Laura Jean. "Recognizing Vulnerability & Oversharing: Can You Be Too Vulnerable?" *Pivot*, January 10, 2023. https://www.lovetopivot.com/how-recognize-vulnerability-signs-overly-vulnerable/.

[23] Manning, Katherine. "We Need Trauma-Informed Workplaces." *Harvard Business Review*, March 31, 2022. https://hbr.org/2022/03/we-need-trauma-informed-workplaces.

[24] LinkedIn. "The Importance of Mentorship in the Workplace: Supporting Growth and Development." January 9, 2024. https://linkedin.com/pulse/importance-mentorship-workplace-supporting-growth-development-5pipc/.

[25] Lyda Hill Institute for Human Resilience. "Empowering Survivors: The Vital Role of Trauma-Informed Mentorship." February 7, 2024. https://resilience.uccs.edu/node/2450/latest.

[26] Lyman, Alex. "It's a Two-Way Street: Four Ways Mentoring Benefits the Mentor." *The Chronicle of Evidence-Based Mentoring*. https://evidencebasedmentoring.org/four-ways-mentoring-benefits-mentor/.

[27] *Psychology Today*. "How to Grow Your Tolerance for Uncertainty." April 2024. https://psychologytoday.com/us/blog/unpacking-anxiety/202404/how-to-grow-your-tolerance-for-uncertainty.

[28] Brigham Young University. "Study Visually Captures Hard Truth: Walking Home At Night Is Not The Same For Women." February 6, 2024. https://news.byu.edu/intellect/study-visually-captures-hard-truth-walking-home-at-night-is-not-the-same-for-women.

[29] Sierra, Cassandra. "Analyzing Gender Differences in Stress Responses." *Heal Behavioral Health*, May 30, 2024. https://healtreatmentcenters.com/mental-health/gender-differences-stress/.

[30] Alam, Nafees. "How Rigid Gender Roles Create Stress: True Fair-

ness Means Valuing People Beyond Achievement or Appearance." *Psychology Today*, February 19, 2025. https://psychologytoday.com/us/blog/pop-culture-mental-health/202502/the-double-standard-in-heteronormative-relationships.

[31] Munir, Muhammad. "Men and Stress: A Silent Struggle." *Talkspace*, October 23, 2024. https://talkspace.com/blog/men-and-stress/.

[32] Babajide, Ronke. "Why There's No Room for Women's Emotions in the Workplace." *LinkedIn*, January 16, 2022. https://linkedin.com/pulse/why-theres-room-womens-emotions-workplace-ronke-babajide-dr-/.

[33] Jones, Andreas. "Why Leadership Stress Is on the Rise — and How to Fight Back." *Entrepreneur*, April 23, 2025. https://entrepreneur.com/leadership/leadership-stress-is-on-the-rise-heres-how-to-fight-back/487864.

[34] Alfaro, Ricardo. "Are There Differences Between Female and Male Leadership?" *Managers Lab*. https://managerslab.com/en/are-there-differences-between-female-and-male-leadership/.

[35] US Department of Veterans Affairs. "Grief: Helping Someone Else After a Loss." March 26, 2025. https://ptsd.va.gov/family/how_help_grief.asp.

[36] Reham, Asma. "Things Never To Say To Trauma Survivors." *Grief Recovery Center*. https://griefrecoveryhouston.com/things-never-to-say-to-trauma-survivors/.

[37] Wikipedia. "2017 Las Vegas Shooting." https://en.wikipedia.org/wiki/2017_Las_Vegas_shooting.

[38] Allison, Scott T. "5 Surprising Ways That Heroes Improve Our Lives." *Psychology Today*, April 16, 2014. https://psychologytoday.com/us/blog/why-we-need-heroes/201404/5-surprising-ways-that-heroes-improve-our-lives.

[39] The Associated Press. "For Route 91 Survivors, 'Country Strong' Means Community." *Fox17*, September 28, 2018. https://fox17.com/news/local/for-route-91-survivors-country-strong-means-community.

[40] Whitney, Caroline. "7 Reasons Your Company Should Arrange a Staff Retreat." *Justworks*, November 3, 2017. https://justworks.com/blog/team-bonding-ideas-7-reasons-arrange-staff-retreat.

[41] Brean, Henry and Rachel Crosby. "91 Points of Light in Las Vegas' Darkest Hour: Humanity Shone Brightly." *Legal Aid Center*, September 30, 2018. https://lacsn.org/who-we-are/legal-aid-in-the-news/91-points-of-light-in-las-vegas-darkest-hour-humanity-shone-brightly.

ABOUT THE AUTHOR

Carly Fliesher is a wife, mother of two and the senior vice president of enterprise sales at Openforce and technology chair for the Express Carriers Association. A survivor of the Route 91 Harvest festival mass shooting, Fliesher became determined to transform her trauma into purpose. While developing frameworks for supporting employees through crises, she also advanced her career from a small startup that was acquired by Walmart to a role in executive leadership.

For more information about Carly Fliesher,
scan the QR code below:

ABOUT THE PUBLISHER

Legacy Launch Pad is a boutique publishing company that works with entrepreneurs from all over the world.

For more information about Legacy Launch Pad Publishing, go to: www.legacylaunchpadpub.com.

www.ingramcontent.com/pod-product-compliance
Lightning Source LLC
Chambersburg PA
CBHW030454210326
41597CB00013B/660